OTHER BOOKS IN ENGLISH BY GEORGE GÖMÖRI

Polish and Hungarian Poetry 1945 to 1956

Cyprian Norwid

The Colonnade of Teeth: Modern Hungarian Poetry,
edited with George Szirtes

Eternal Monday: New and Selected Poems (György Petri's
poems), translated with Clive Wilmer

Magnetic Poles: Essays on Polish and Comparative Literature

Forced March (Miklós Radnóti's selected poems),
translated with Clive Wilmer

Polishing October (George Gömöri's selected poems),
translated with Clive Wilmer

I Lived on this Earth... Hungarian Poets on the Holocaust,
edited with Mari Gömöri

*Polish Swan Triumphant: Essays on Polish and Comparative
Literature*

The Alien in
the Chapel

Ferenc Békássy

Rupert Brooke's Unknown Rival

Poems and Letters
Edited by George Gömöri and Mari Gömöri
Epilogue by Peter Jones

SKYSCRAPER

Published by Skyscraper Publications Limited
20 Crab Tree Close, Bloxham, OX15 4SE
www.skyscraperpublications.com

First published in 2016

A CIP catalogue record for this book is available
from the British Library.

ISBN-13: 978-0-9931533-9-6

Cover concept and design
by Grace Fussell

Typesetting by
Chandler Book Design

Printed in Cesky Tesin by Finidr

*Ferenc Békássy, on graduating from King's College,
Cambridge, 1914*

CONTENTS

ILLUSTRATIONS

ACKNOWLEDGEMENTS

I n the first instance we are grateful to the late Angela Harris, Noel Olivier's daughter, who some years ago gave her permission for the publication of Ferenc Békássy's letters to her mother. We would like to thank Tamsin Majerus, Angela's daughter, who continued to support the project, providing copies of the original letters and answering with patience our many queries and who together with her younger sister Dame Pippa Harris, gave us permission to use the two photos of Noel and the one of Noel and her sisters. We are indebted to Dame Pippa Harris, editor of *Song of Love. The Letters of Rupert Brooke to Noel Olivier*, a book which was of enormous help to us and clarified many points about Noel's relationships. We also thank her for permission to reproduce one of Noel's letters to Brooke.

On the Békássy family side, Zsófia Farkas, granddaughter of Ferenc Békássy's oldest sister Antonia, was a great help in providing us with much information and we thank her for her interest and assistance. Tamás Békássy provided useful information on his great uncle, János Békássy, Ferenc Békássy's brother. Thanks are due also to Gábor Görgey, for information on his aunt, Antonia Békássy.

Special thanks are due to Tibor Sennyey Weiner, editor of *Békássy Ferenc egybegyűjtött írásai* (Ferenc Békássy's Collected Writings) which provided useful data on Békássy's work.

We are grateful to Elizabeth Hollingsworth for providing the two letters to her father Justin Brooke. Richard and Henrietta Garnett provided the two letters to Constance Garnett. These are now deposited in the Northwestern University Library and thanks are due to Nick Munagian at the library for answering our queries.

We would like to thank the Provost and the Scholars of King's College, Cambridge for permission to reproduce Békássy's letters to J. M. Keynes and J. T. Sheppard. We also thank them for permission to reproduce the photograph of King's College and the photographs of Ferenc Békássy, Rupert Brooke and John Maynard Keynes. We also thank Patricia McGuire of the Archive Centre, King's College, Cambridge, for all her assistance, as well as the Manuscript Department of the British Library, Robin Darwall-Smith of University College, Oxford, and Anne Thomson of Newnham College, Cambridge. Jane Kirby, Archivist at Bedales school also provided substantial information and we thank her.

Thanks are due also to Eszter Simon of the Artist's Retreat at Zsennye, housed in the old home of the Békássy family, for providing the photos of Zsennye Castle.

The excerpt from Gordon Luce's letter to John Maynard Keynes is reproduced by the kind permission of his family.

We are also very grateful to Peter Sherwood, György Pauk, Lynn Hieatt and Conrad Guettler for their help with various queries we had while preparing our book. Particular thanks are due to Zoltán Sumonyi, with whom we have spent many enjoyable hours discussing various aspects of Békássy's life and work.

Above all we would like to thank Peter Jones, Librarian and Fellow of King's College, Cambridge and who wrote the Epilogue, for putting us in touch with Karl Sabbagh of Skyscraper Publications and championing this whole project. Karl Sabbagh, a Kingsman himself, was enthusiastic about the book from the start and has encouraged us, has had great patience with us and his help and editing of this volume have been invaluable.

EDITORS' NOTES

A ll of Ferenc Békássy's known letters to Noel Olivier are reproduced in this book, (though a couple are just summarised), as are all known letters to John Maynard Keynes. There are two letters to James Strachey, but we have decided not to include the brief notes sent to him by Békássy. All extant letters to the other recipients, namely Justin Brooke, Constance Garnett and John T. Sheppard are included. There is one letter to Raisley Moorsom, also in the King's Archives Centre, which we have omitted.

We have standardised and formatted the dates and greetings and have changed Békássy's prodigious use of '&' to 'and' and '&tc' to 'etc'. We have standardised the many hyphens and dashes that appear in the originals. Where no dates appear on the letters themselves, we have used the postmark from the envelopes. Where these did not exist, or where the postmark was illegible we have made an intelligent guess of the time of writing. All of these as well as inserts by us are indicated by square brackets. In one letter where Békássy himself has used a square bracket, we have changed it to the following: '{ }'. Where words are underlined, on the whole we have italicised them. Foreign words and phrases we have italicised and translated in the footnotes. Where these are quotes from literary works, the sources also appear in the footnotes. In several letters, Békássy himself used footnotes. These are marked [F.B.note]. Occasionally Békássy misspells a name, or in the case of Jacques Raverat, uses both spellings of the first name (Jaques and Jacques). We have not corrected these, neither have we corrected some idiosyncrasies of Békássy's use of the English language. Where Békássy has crossed something out in the letter, we have omitted it if it was illegible, but left the crossing out where the words could be made out. We have taken the liberty to make a few minor corrections, mainly of punctuation in the letters, for the purposes of clarification.

We have edited some of the letters to Noel where there are repetitions, or where we felt the material was not of interest and these are indicated by ellipses: [...].

As Noel's own letters to Békássy have sadly not survived, in order to hear her 'voice' we have included one of her letters to Rupert Brooke.

We have made a list of those names which crop up regularly under the heading Main Characters. When these names occur in the Introduction or in a letter the first time, there is a footnote about them, but not thereafter. Minor characters are identified in the footnotes the first time they appear, after that only if there is some additional information relating to them.

Throughout the correspondence with a couple of exceptions Békássy uses his surname in his signature and addresses Noel and her sisters and friends from Bedales by their first name. We use the same form of the names both in our Introduction and in the footnotes. The male characters he refers to either by their first name, surname or their nickname. Occasionally for clarification we have inserted in square brackets the surname, where only the first name appears.

The first time a publication is mentioned the footnote gives full title and details of author and publisher. After that the following abbreviations are used:

Song of Love - SONG OF LOVE, The Letters of Rupert Brooke and Noel Olivier 1909-1915

Nigel Jones - RUPERT BROOKE, Life, Death & Myth

Friends & Apostles - Friends & Apostles, The Correspondence of Rupert Brooke and James Strachey 1905-1914

Sennyey Weiner - Békássy Ferenc egybegyűjtött írásai

BL - The British Library, London

ACKC - Archive Centre King's College, Cambridge

MAIN CHARACTERS

Ferenc Békássy's Family

István Békássy - father, landowner, Lord Lieutenant (*Főispán*) of Vas County, (1863-1932)

Emma Békássy née Bezerédj, (Bezerédy) - mother, translator and literary critic, (1865-1944)

Antonia (Tónika) Békássy - sister, educated at Bedales and Slade Art School, London, returned to Hungary, married József Görgey, Officer of a Hussar regiment in 1913, (1889-1978)

Ferenc (Feri) Békássy educated at Bedales school and Cambridge, (1893-1915)

John (János) Békássy - brother, educated at Bedales, interned in 1914, settled in England, married Rosamund Wedgewood in 1920, (1894-1983)

Stephen (István) Békássy - brother, educated at Bedales and Switzerland, returned to Hungary, (1896-1974)

Éva Békássy - sister, educated at Bedales continued her studies in Switzerland, (1898-1997)

Klára Békássy - sister, educated at Bedales, returned to Hungary at the outbreak of war, (1901-1989)

Flóra Békássy - cousin on father's side. Two years at Bedales. Returned to Hungary, (1893-?)

Ilona Duczynska - cousin on father's side, author and translator, spent the war years in Switzerland. Married Karl Polányi. (1897-1978)

Noel Olivier's Family

Sir Sidney Olivier (Baron Olivier of Ramsden) - father. Leading Fabian figure, Governor-General of Jamaica, (1859-1943)

Margery Olivier - sister, studied at Newnham College, Cambridge, (1886-1974)

Brynhild Olivier (Bryn) - sister, married Hugh Popham in 1912. (1887-1935)

Daphne Olivier - sister, studied at Newnham College, Cambridge, (1889-1950)

Noel Olivier - attended Bedales, studied medicine at University College, London, (1892-1969)

Friends and teachers at Bedales School

John Hayden Badley (The Chief) - Founder and Headmaster, (1865-1967)

Helen Thomas - teacher at Bedales

Edward Thomas - poet and critic, married to Helen Thomas. (1878-1917)

Elliot Logwood (Peter) Grant-Watson - Australian writer, educated at Bedales, where he later taught. Resided for a while in London and also rented Rupert Brooke's lodgings at the

Old Vicarage Grantchester in 1913-14, when Brooke was in America and Tahiti, (1885-1970)

Raisley Moorsom - educated at Bedales and King's College, Cambridge. Kept detailed diaries for many years, now in King's College Archives, (1892 -1981)

John Hugo Gotch - educated at Bedales and went up to Cambridge the year before Békássy

Justin Brooke - together with Rupert Brooke (no relation), founded in 1907 The Marlowe Society in Cambridge, (1885-1963)

Cambridge Friends and Acquaintances

Rupert Brooke - poet, educated at Rugby and King's College, Cambridge. Member of the Apostles in 1908 and Fellow of King's from 1913, (1887-1915)

John Maynard Keynes - economist, Fellow, later Bursar of King's College, member of the Apostles, (1883-1946)

George Edward (G.E.) Moore - philosopher author of *Principia Ethica* (1903), member of the Apostles, (1873-1958)

Bertrand Russell - philosopher, Fellow of Trinity College, member of the Apostles, (1872-1970)

Lytton Strachey - writer, member of the Apostles and one of the founders of the Bloomsbury Group, (1880-1932)

James Strachey - writer, educated at Trinity College, Cambridge, member of the Apostles and Bloomsbury Group, (1887-1967)

Ludwig Wittgenstein - Austrian philosopher, member of the Apostles and later Fellow of Trinity College, (1889-1951)

Frank Bliss - fellow student at King's College, member of the Apostles, killed in World War I, in 1916

Francis Cornford - classical scholar, (1874-1943)

Frances Cornford (née Darwin) - poet, married to Francis Cornford, (1886-1960)

Jacques Raverat - French painter, educated at Bedales and King's College, Cambridge, (1885-1925)

Gwen Raverat (née Darwin) - wood engraver, married to Jacques Raverat, (1885-1957)

Goldsworthy (Goldie) Lowes Dickinson - classical philologist, Fellow of King's College. Friend of John Badley, Headmaster of Bedales, member of the Apostles, (1862-1932)

Gordon (Lucy) Luce - student at Emmanuel College, Cambridge. Elected to the Apostles together with Békássy, settled in Burma, (1889-1979). In 1923 Hogarth Press published a volume of his verse, called *Poems*.

Frank Laurence (Peter) Lucas - classical philologist, Student at Trinity, later Fellow of King's College, member of the Apostles, (1894-1967)

Gerald Frank Shove - economist, student and later Fellow of King's College, member of the Apostles, (1887-1947)

John Tressider Sheppard - Fellow, later Provost of King's College, member of the Apostles, (1881-1968)

INTRODUCTION

On the wall of the All Souls Memorial Chapel in King's College Chapel, Cambridge, there is a plaque commemorating members of the college who died in action during the First World War. The second name is that of Rupert Brooke. At right angles on a separate wall, there is a small plaque with a single name on it, that of Ferenc Békássy, a young Hungarian, a published poet already during his short lifetime. He was a love rival of Rupert Brooke and like Brooke died fighting in the war, though on the opposite side.

We hope this volume of his correspondence and poems will shed light on this 'alien', someone who was welcomed by the leading intellectuals and thinkers of contemporary Cambridge, such as John Maynard Keynes and G.E. Moore, as well as by members of the Bloomsbury group including Lytton and James Strachey.

Ferenc István Dénes Gyula Békássy (known as Ferenc or Feri) was born on April 7th 1893, in Kis-Sennye,[1] Western Hungary, the second child of István and Emma Békássy,

---

[1] Present-day Zsennye.

Békássy's family home at Zsennye, in Hungary

née Bezerédj,[2] into an upper-class landowning noble family, which, though not belonging to the super-rich aristocracy, was very well off. Hungary at this time was part of the Austro-Hungarian Monarchy. In 1848, when Hungary failed to attain independence from the Austrian Empire by political means, a long armed struggle followed but was eventually suppressed by the Austrians with the military assistance of the Russian Army. After an absolutist rule was imposed on Hungary by Austria, a compromise was reached in 1867 and the Emperor Franz Joseph was crowned King of Hungary, giving the country a limited independence. Although the country was industrialised by the time Ferenc Békássy was born, the landowning classes on the whole retained their land and accustomed way of life.

The Békássy's main residence, a castle at Kis-Sennye,[3] where

---

[2]   Present-day spelling Bezerédy.
[3]   The castle was refurbished in 2015 and is now a state-funded Retreat for Artists.

the six children, (the seventh having died in infancy), were brought up was in fact part of Emma Bezerédj's dowry. The park in which the castle stood had been landscaped by Emma's grandfather and was surrounded by rivers and brooks. The Békássy children were encouraged to roam freely, retaining a lifelong love of nature.

It appears that Emma was the more intellectual partner in the relationship. The castle had a library of nearly 3000 books[4] and the children learnt languages and read widely. At the same time as bringing up her children Emma translated from English and French. After World War I she wrote reviews of English books for Hungary's leading cultural magazine, *Nyugat* (West).[5] Though not a domineering woman, her influence on the children, in particular on her eldest son Ferenc, was strong, and it was she who decided to send all of them to Bedales, a newly established boarding school in England. The school, one of the first which was co-educational in England, was founded by Cambridge-educated John Haden Badley in 1893 and located at Lindfield, moving a few years later to Steep near Petersfield and was one of the leading experimental British educational establishments of the time. An enthusiastic supporter of the school was a Frenchman, Edmond Demolins, whose son was at the school and who extolled the virtues of English public schools in two publications, citing Bedales as the finest example (*A quoi tient la supériorité des Anglo-Saxon and L'Éducation nouvelle*).[6] Emma Békássy, having read these, decided to send Antonia, her first-born, to Bedales. Antonia flourished at the school and Ferenc Békássy followed her in the autumn term of 1905 at the age of twelve.

---

[4] Of these only 500 survived but have been distributed amongst the relatives. Éva Békássy remembered Russian soldiers in 1945 ransacking the castle (as told to Zsófia Farkas, her great-niece).

[5] Under the pen-name Magdolna Rosti, she wrote reviews of Vita Sackville-West, Lytton Strachey, Virginia Woolf and other English writers.

[6] *'To what do the Anglo Saxons owe their superiority?'* and *'New Education'.*

He would have spoken some English already and made
quick progress at the school. He was precocious and well-
read in German and French as well as in his mother tongue.
By the age of sixteen his English was such that he began to
write poetry in English as well as in Hungarian. It was during
this time that he began earnestly to record impressions of the
books he was reading and to write essays, some of which, e.g.
one on Nietzsche, were published in the school magazine,
Bedales Chronicle.[7] There were writers on both sides of his large
and distinguished family; Amália, the sister of his maternal
grandfather Elek Bezerédj is remembered as the author of the
first children's book in Hungarian[8] and Békássy's aunt, Helen
Békássy, his father's sister-in-law, published several books of
poetry.[9] His cousin Flóra (who also attended Bedales for two
years), wrote a novel which was never published, but which she
read to Békássy.[10]

During his years at Bedales, Békássy made lifelong friends,
the most important and meaningful relationship being that with
Noel Olivier, with whom he corresponded regularly from 1911
(while he was still at the school) until a few weeks before his
death in 1915. Noel, born in 1892, was the youngest daughter
of Margaret Cox and Sir Sydney Olivier, later Baron Olivier
of Ramsden, a politician and one of the first members of the
Fabian Society, (founded in 1884) which promoted radical social
reform. He made his career in the British Colonial Service and
became Governor-General of Jamaica in 1907. Back in England
temporarily in 1908 he built the family home, 'The Champions'
at Limpsfield Chart in Sussex, in an area popular with other
Fabian families, whose children remained close with the Olivier

[7] Friedrich Nietzsche (1844 -1900) German philosopher. *Bedales Chronicle*, Vol.3, 30
   October 1909.
[8] *Flóri könyve* (The Book of Flori) published posthumously in 1839-840.
[9] The second collection, as sentimental as the first, was published in 1906.
[10] Békássy to Noel Olivier, Bicske, 5 September 1913.

children as they grew up. Though two of the older Olivier daughters went to Cambridge, according to David Garnett a writer friend who had known the family as a child, Noel was the most intelligent: "Noel alone of the four developed a mind which was courageous, realistic and profound."[11] She became a boarder at Bedales in 1908, three years after Békássy.

In 1908, when she was just 15, Noel accompanied her father on a visit to Cambridge, and it was here at a Fabian Society dinner in his honour that she caught the eye of Rupert Brooke, an undergraduate at King's, already an acknowledged poet. Brooke was immediately smitten and launched a torrent of letters to her avowing his love. Despite the persistent tone of Brooke's letters Noel, who was according to all who knew her, very restrained and "unusually unemotional", never allowed the relationship to develop beyond the platonic, though according to Brooke she agreed to a secret engagement,[12] something she later denied.[13] Their long-lasting correspondence *Song of Love* was edited by Pippa Harris, Noel's granddaughter, and published in 1991.

The correspondence between Békássy and Noel began in earnest in 1911 when, after finishing Bedales, Békássy returned to Hungary. He came back to England in the autumn to read History at King's College, Cambridge, while Noel enrolled in University College, London to read medicine.

From this one-sided correspondence, (sadly Noel's letters have not survived), a picture emerges of Békássy as a highly intelligent, well-read, sensitive young man, who spoke several languages like a native. His feelings for Noel are unwavering.

---

[11] David Garnett, *The Golden Echo*, Chatto and Windus, London, 1953, p.181.

[12] Rupert Brooke and Noel's secret engagement took place allegedly at a summer camp at Beaulieu in 1910, Christopher Hassall, *Rupert Brooke: A Biography*, London, Faber and Faber, 1964, p.230. Also quoted by Paul Delany, *The Neo-Pagans*, London, 1987, p. 91.

[13] Hassall, quoted by Keith Hale ed. *Friends & Apostles, The Correspondence of Rupert Brooke and James Strachey (1905-1914)*, Yale University Press, New York and London, 1998, p. 91.

He is constantly yearning for more intimacy and for more of Noel's time, but just as with her response to Brooke, Noel keeps him at arms length calling being in love an "illness".[14] However, in both cases she willingly continues the correspondence and must have been deeply flattered by the attention of these two erudite young poets, even playing one off against the other.

In August 1911, while Noel was at summer camp at Clifford Bridge with a group of friends including Brooke, she received a letter from Békássy who was back in Hungary. It was the first time he had spoken of his deep feelings for her.[15] Noel showed this letter to Brooke,[16] and she managed to arouse Brooke's curiosity in light of the fact that Békássy too was a poet, and, even more to the point, would be going up to Cambridge to Brooke's old college, King's.

Once in Cambridge, Békássy's letters to Noel are full of information about his new acquaintances, many of whom were homosexual. Of those befriending him, the one who made the greatest impression was the economist and Fellow of King's College, John Maynard Keynes, who took him under his wing. At first in a letter to his partner Duncan Grant,[17] Keynes calls Békássy 'the Hun'[18] later referring to him by his first name Ferenc, finally by his nickname Feri. He soon became fond of this exceptionally intelligent first-year student and was instrumental in having him elected to the *Conversazione Society*. Better known as the Apostles, it was founded in 1820, an exclusive debating society of undergraduates and Fellows meeting regularly on Saturdays. At any one time there could

---

[14] Pippa Harris ed. *Song of Love. The Letters of Rupert Brooke and Noel Olivier 1909-1915*, Bloomsbury, London, 1991, p. 91.

[15] Békássy to Noel 23 August 1911.

[16] Nigel Jones, *Rupert Brooke, Life, Death & Myth*, Richard Cohen Books, London, 1999, p. 202.

[17] Duncan Grant (1885 -1978) painter, lover of John Maynard Keynes.

[18] Keynes to Grant, 5 January, 1912, Keynes Papers, Vol III, BL, MS Add. 57931, f.1.

only be twelve current members elected from undergraduates. Once elected, however, ex-members known as 'Angels' had lifelong rights to attend meetings and to put forward names of new candidates who were referred to as 'embryos'. In 1911 the 'Angels' included such illustrious names as the philosophers G.E. Moore and Bertrand Russell, the classicist G.L. Dickinson, the essayist Lytton Strachey and of course Rupert Brooke.

Keynes asked Lytton Strachey's younger brother James, an 'Angel' now working in London, to put Békássy's name forward in January 1912. James Strachey in a letter to Rupert Brooke describes Békássy's reaction to being told of the possibility of his election: "he took it like a fish [and] wolfed it down, [...] he found the whole thing fitting him [. . .]like a glove". In his next letter to Brooke, Strachey reports that at the meeting when he was duly elected, Békássy was "wildly excited and remarkably intelligent".[19] Apart from Keynes, Békássy was the only first-year student to have been elected to the Apostles. He was also the first foreigner.

He was followed a few months later by another foreigner, the Austrian philosopher Ludwig Wittgenstein. This came as no surprise to Békássy who knew of Wittgenstein's reputation and had written in one of his letters to Noel about "the Austrian" who is so clever that "he utterly confounds Russell and Moore".[20]

Keynes, being homosexual, may have had ulterior motives for his friendship with the young 'Hun', but eventually came to accept the role of a benevolent older friend and confidant. In a letter of February 1912, Keynes reveals in a letter to Duncan Grant that Békássy told him about loving several people at the same time.[21] One of these was obviously Noel, the other one can

---

[19] James Strachey to Rupert Brooke, 29 January 1912, *Friends & Apostles*, p.217-219. On the same subject Keynes to Grant: "As you have probably heard we elected Luce and Békássy on Saturday. The birth was wonderful, easy…" Keynes, Vol III, BL, MS Add. 57931, f.3.

[20] Békássy to Noel, 5 May 1912.

[21] Keynes to Grant, February 1912, Keynes, Vol III, BL, MS Add. 57931, f.9.

be surmised from one of James Strachey's letters to his brother Lytton, in which he says Békássy confessed to him that "It [his feelings for Noel] runs in parallel lines with [...] feelings towards Bliss".[22] Frank Bliss was a handsome, athletic classicist and fellow-Kingsman who according to Keynes "had a dreadful effect on Feri's character"[23] though this may just have been jealousy on Keynes's part. Despite Békássy finding himself so at home in Cambridge within what was predominantly a homosexual circle of friends, and despite his attraction to Bliss, it appears that all of his relationships remained platonic.

Békássy's life soon settled into a new routine. Term-time was spent in Cambridge, while most holidays he travelled home to the family estate or visited other European countries, Switzerland being a favourite. He also visited his old school Bedales frequently and kept in touch with his many friends from there. One in particular, Elliot Logwood Grant-Watson, known to his friends as Peter, who had taught there for a while, eventually became one of his closest friends. He was also forging new friendships amongst the Cambridge elite, namely with the poet Frances Cornford (née Darwin) and the painters Gwen and Jacques Raverat.

Despite these new friends and though feeling very much at home amongst the Apostles, Békássy in his first year at King's must still have felt very much an outsider. Even his friend James Strachey mocks his accent and refers to him as 'the foreigner'.[24] To show appreciation for Keynes's support in having him elected to the Apostles, and no doubt to impress his bourgeois mentor, Békássy invited him for a visit to his family home in Hungary.[25]

[22] James Strachey to Lytton Strachey, 1 November 1912. Paul Delany, *The Neo-Pagans*, p.143.

[23] Keynes to Grant, 4 June 1912, Keynes, Vol III, BL, MS Add.57931, f.24.

[24] James Strachey to Rupert Brooke, 26 January 1912, *Friends & Apostles*, p. 215.

[25] Békássy to James Strachey, Schluderbach, 5 September 1912, Strachey Papers, BL, MS Add. 60568, f.1.

Keynes accepted the invitation, his two week-long visit taking place in the second half of September 1912. On the whole he enjoyed his stay in Hungary where the contrast between the lifestyle of the landowners and the living conditions of peasants reminded him of a Russia, known to him from the novels of Tolstoy "though on a much smaller scale".[26] It surprised him that so many of the elite of the Austro-Hungarian Monarchy spoke English, and resented the fact that despite this, his hosts often changed to the impenetrable Hungarian in his presence.[27] The youngest Békássy daughter, Klára, recalled her mother describing Keynes "sitting silent at a big dinner party in the house, unable to understand a word, and watching the hands of all the guests. After they had gone, said my mother, he gave her a short account of the character of each of them as he had observed from their hands, and he was astoundingly right."[28]

Back in Cambridge during his second year, Békássy continued to enjoy the social and intellectual opportunities it offered. He worked hard during his years at King's, and wrote a number of perceptive essays, one of which (on Robert Browning) won a Prize in his College. As for his poetry, he wrote alternately in English and Hungarian, often writing two versions of the same poem, rather than translating one to the other. Because he read poetry in English, Latin, French, German and of course Hungarian, it is not only Keats, Browning, Walter de la Mare or even (ironically) Rupert Brooke who influenced him, but also André Gide, Jules Laforgue and later Rainer Maria Rilke. Apart from these poets, Békássy also identified with the modern poetry movement taking shape in Hungary and in fact sent some of his poems to one of its leading exponents, Mihály Babits, hoping for approval, which unfortunately he did not get.

---

[26] Keynes to Grant,19 September, 1912, Keynes, Vol.III, BL, MS Add. 57931, f. 34.

[27] ibid. f.35.

[28] István Gál, *The New Hungarian Quarterly*, No.49 (Spring 1971), p.189.

After Békássy's death however, in his moving obituary Babits expresses regret at having written back negatively as "had he lived, he could have become a very great Hungarian poet".[29]

Békássy had more success with the poems he wrote in English and two were accepted for publication in the June 1913 issue of King's own magazine, *Basileon*. His poems were well received and together with the work of several other Kingsmen, two of his other poems were chosen for inclusion in the anthology *Cambridge Poets 1900-1913*, edited by Aelfrida Tillyard, (herself a poet) and subedited by another Cambridge poet Frank W. Stokoe. Aelfrida Tillyard had met Békássy earlier and they had formed a favourable opinion of each other.[30] While the poems in this anthology are of varying quality, including far too many by the neo-Pagan Aleister Crowley, it also contains Rupert Brooke's legendary poem 'The Old Vicarage, Grantchester' as well as Frances Cornford's admiring, but critical epigram 'Youth', comparing Rupert Brooke to 'a young Apollo' unprepared for life.[31]

From the moment back in 1911 when Noel had teased him with Békássy's letter, Brooke - as mentioned - had been curious to make the acquaintance of his rival and made sure that he looked Békássy up as soon as he could. His first impression was not unfavourable and in a letter to Noel giving an account of this meeting he says: "he is, being not-English, the only decent person in Cambridge." He continues in a characteristic fashion "They [meaning his other Cambridge friends] all loathe me."[32] His attitude to Békássy went through phases ranging from jealousy to

---

[29]   Mihály Babits, *Nyugat*, 1915/2. p.824. Also in Mihály Babits, *Irodalmi emlékek*, Budapest, 1917, p. 285.

[30]   Békássy to Noel, 18 May 1913, also Sheila Mann, *Aelfrida Tillyard, Hints of a Perfect Splendour. A Novel Biography* [Cambridge], 2013, p. 211.

[31]   *Cambridge Poets 1900-1913, An Anthology*, Cambridge, W. Heffer and Sons Ltd., 1913, pp.25-30, and p.42. One of the reviewers, Edward Thomas, singled out Békássy's poems for praise, cf. *Poetry and Drama*, December 1913.

[32]   *Song of Love*, p.138.

grudging acceptance and finally to a certain respect for his poetry, though in a letter to James Strachey he says electing 'Farry' to the Apostles "is the maddest thing I ever heard of."[33] In several of his letters to Noel he mockingly refers to him as 'Signior' Békássy.[34] Békássy on his part, was not jealous of Brooke, merely curious of 'Rupert's' exploits, frequently asking Noel for news of him and at one point warning her with the words "Rupert is grand (at a safe distance)... but dangerous!"[35] At one point Békássy sent some of his poems to the seemingly friendly Brooke and was gravely disappointed when they were returned without any comment. As Brooke explained to Noel later in his letter of 28 January 1913, "Yes: I knew about Békássy. He went off to stay a weekend with you in the Autumn term... I'd just then got rather fond of him, and - for instance - he'd sent me his poems to read; and of course, I immediately hated him, and sent his poems back without comment."[36] An unresentful Békássy, on the other hand, writing to Noel, mentions Brooke visiting Cambridge on the occasion of picking up his M.A. and dining for the first time as Fellow, at High Table in King's College.[37]

During his final academic year (1913/1914) Békássy concentrated on studying towards his degree. He read voraciously, wrote papers, attended the influential Greek scholar 'Goldie' Dickinson's seminars on English literature, yet still managed to socialise, at one point visiting Jacques and Gwen Raverat who had moved out to a remote spot near Royston in Cambridgeshire.[38] One of his essays from this time was a perceptive analysis of modern Hungarian poetry which included several of his own

---

[33] Rupert Brooke to James Strachey, [27 January1912], *Friends & Apostles*, p. 217.

[34] *Song of Love*, p.139 et al.

[35] Békássy to Noel, Cambridge, 22 October 1912.

[36] *Song of Love*, p. 229.

[37] Békássy to Noel, King's. [26 April 1913]

[38] Békássy to Noel, Cambridge, 6 March ,1913, published in *The Hungarian Quarterly*, No.199 (Autumn 2010), pp. 110-112.

translations of leading Hungarian poets. Apparently, he sent this essay to the short-lived literary quarterly *Poetry and Drama*. It is possible that it was accepted for publication, but due perhaps to the outbreak of hostilities in 1914, when Békássy officially became an alien, his essay never made it to print.[39]

In one of the last letters of 1913 to Noel, he writes that he will have to leave England after his finals, to serve a compulsory year in the Austro-Hungarian army. It is in this context that we have to understand the following sentence: "I am shaking off one after another, the shackles which bind me to England".[40] One of those 'shackles' must have been his emotional attachment to Noel, something he never did shake off. The tone of his letters during his last term in 1914, despite the fact that Noel rejected him and wished to communicate via letters only, become more pleading, and despite the evidence to the contrary he still believes that "we belong together".[41] In fact earlier that year Noel had written to Rupert Brooke that despite the fact that Békássy "was wonderfully nice" and "probably superior to anyone I knew [...] I - in my zeal - tried to induce Békássy to become a stranger." Though she says "Békássy is of[f] my time", they met again more than once.[42]

In June 1914 having attained a II/1 in his finals and prior to returning to Hungary for good, he went to spend a few weeks at Château d'Oex by Lake Lucerne in Switzerland in the company of his close friend 'Peter' Grant-Watson.[43] It was during this holiday

---

[39] Elemér Békássy, Ferenc Békássy's uncle, as quoted in Tibor Sennyei Weiner ed. *Békássy Ferenc egybegyűjtött írásai*, (Ferenc Békássy's Collected Writings) Aranymadár Alapítvány-Irodalmi Jelen, Budapest-Zsennye, 2010, p.440, assumes that the essay did get published in *Poetry and Drama*, and that the original English MS remained in Cambridge.

[40] Békássy to Noel, Cambridge, 1 November 1913.

[41] Békássy to Noel 23 June 1914.

[42] *Song of Love*, p. 260.

[43] Château d'Oex was where the parents of Grant-Watson, Oswald and Lucy Powell had set up a small tutorial college, Suzanne Falkiner, *The Imago. E.L. Grant-Watson & Australia*, UWA Publishing, Crawley, Western Australia, 2011, p.226.

that news of the assassination of Archduke Franz Ferdinand on the 28th of June reached them. According to Grant-Watson, Békássy was aware that the Austro-Hungarian Monarchy was mobilising and realised that they would soon be at war with Russia, a country whose culture his friend respected but whose military power he feared.[44] In July Békássy returned to England, presumably to collect his belongings, then proceeded to Hungary. He knew he would be called up soon, but at his mother's bidding returned to England once more to collect his younger sisters who were still at Bedales. He just managed to do this, as though England was already at war with Germany, it did not declare war on the Austro-Hungarian Monarchy until August 12th. As the banks in England were closed, Békássy had to enlist Keynes' help to obtain funds for his journey home. Keynes tried to convince him to stay in England but when that failed provided the money.[45]

In the end Békássy collected only Klára the younger sister, Éva deciding to stay for one more term at Bedales.[46] Back in Hungary he continued to write poems, though mainly in Hungarian. He was called up in late August to one of the Hussar Regiments and received his military training at Pápa, in Western Hungary. (Sándor Ferenczi, analyst and disciple of Sigmund Freud, served there as Troop, later Chief Physician at the same time.)[47] The later poems, some written at Pápa, are dominated by reflections on nature, and the sadness of autumn and death. He sent one entitled 'The Year' to his

---

[44] Peter Grant -Watson, *But to What Purpose*, Cresset Press, London,1946, p.156.
[45] Keynes to Duncan Grant, 24 July, 1915, Keynes, Vol.III., BL, MS Add. 57931, f.92. The story of Keynes lending money to Békássy is mentioned by David Garnett in *The Golden Echo*, p. 271.
[46] Roy Wake and Pennie Denton, *Bedales School, The First Hundred Years*, 1893-1993, Haggerston Press, London, 1993, p. 68. (This was the autumn term of 1914, not 1917, as quoted in the book).
[47] Eva Brabant, Ernst Falzeder, Patrizia Giampieri-Deutsch, eds, The *Correspondence of Sigmund Freud and Sándor Ferenczi: 1914-1919*, Harvard University Press, 1993, pp. 19-60.

cousin Ilona Duczynska, who had left Hungary earlier to study in Switzerland. This poem includes a vision of death, which does not seem to hold any fears for the poet, and ends with a self-fulfilling prophecy, *"Hűs hó takarja majd, mely szenvedett,/ Kifáradt, szép, szerelmes testedet"*. (Cool snow will cover your much-suffered/ Exhausted, beautiful, loving body).[48]

In January 1915, having completed his military training, Békássy was waiting to be deployed. As news of ever-increasing casualties on the Russian front reached Hungary, (over 350,000 had died by mid-September the year before), his premonitions of an early death grew stronger. In letters to his friends in England, the memories of his Cambridge years are tinged with nostalgia, as he comes to realise that the idyllic days spent there would never return.

What could this young poet with an allegiance to both his homeland and to England have felt about serving in the war? He had spent his formative years in England forging friendships with some of the most influential thinkers and artists of the time and felt "imbued with Englishness". On other occasions he says that he does not really fit in; "[I] wish I had not[didn't have] to go back to Cambridge. I <u>don't</u> fit in, although I like everybody." But he no longer fitted in at home in Hungary either. He writes to Noel that he is suffocated by the provincialism of "this benighted land". To Constance Garnett when the war breaks out he writes "I see I am getting stuck in the soil already. It's a deadly place, Hungary, when one likes it so."[49] However ambivalent his feelings about Hungary, there

---

[48] Gömöri György, 'Békássy Ferenc levele Duczynska Ilonához', (Ferenc Békássy's letter to Ilona Duczynska) *Irodalomtörténeti Közlemények*, 2010/1, p.79. Ilona Duczynska (1897-1978) Hungarian revolutionary socialist writer, married economic historian Karl Polányi. A slightly different version of this poem 'Az év (The Year) was included in Sennyey Weiner, pp.47-48.

[49] Békássy to Noel, 21 March 1913 and 23 August 1911. Békássy to Constance Garnett, 29 June 1914, The Charles Deering and McCormick Special Collection, Northwestern Library, Evanston, Illinois, MS 164.

was never any doubt in his mind, that despite everything that England had offered him, he would go back home to serve his country and fulfil his destiny, presumably hoping that he would not come into direct confrontation with the British army.

He accepted the outbreak of war and what it entailed with quiet resignation, with similar feelings to that of his friend Edward Thomas who in his poem 'This No Case of Petty Right or Wrong' states clearly that: "I hate not Germans, nor grow hot/ With love of Englishmen, to please newspapers."[50] The last letter Békássy wrote to Keynes was in January 1915, but Keynes received it only after the war in 1920. In this letter Békássy makes his feelings clear: "I can't write about what I think of the war, and even if I could I would hate to..." and towards the end of the letter he adds an even more revealing sentence: "I suppose in England there is the same idiotic hatred of the inimical nations as here."[51]

His last letter to Noel was written in May 1915, just before his unit was sent to the Russian front, but it was not posted. After his death, his sister Éva sent it on to Noel who was on holiday in neutral Switzerland at the time.[52] It becomes evident from this last letter, that Noel had continued writing to Békássy after the outbreak of war, just as she had continued writing to Brooke up until his death a few months before that of Békássy. Like Keynes and most of their circle both in Cambridge and in London, for instance their artist friends in the Bloomsbury Group, Noel did not share the jingoistic mood of vast numbers of the British public.[53] In this last letter Békássy recalls the past,

---

[50] Edward Thomas, *Selected Poems*, ed. Mathew Hollis, Faber and Faber, London, 2014, p.109.

[51] Békássy to Keynes, 6 January 1915, ACKC, Cambridge, Keynes PP/30/45/5, first published in *The New Hungarian Quarterly*, No.79 (Autumn 1980), pp.168-169.

[52] Éva's covering note of 4 July 1915 is printed in this volume alongside the letter.

[53] According to David Garnett, the Bloomsbury Group were "pacifists almost to a man and woman during the First World War", Sarah Knight, *Bloomsbury's Outsider. A Life of David Garnett*, Bloomsbury Reader, London, 2015, p.107

their friendship and their shared time at Bedales, ending the letter on a nostalgic note "I long to see you... I often think of you. And we shall meet, Noel, shan't we, some day?"[54]

Uncannily, Rupert Brooke ends his last letter to Noel musing about the possibility of direct confrontation with Békássy on the battlefield, weighing up their respective chances of survival. He ends his letter with the words, "dreadful if you lose all your lovers at once. - Ah, but you won't lose all -" [55] Sadly that is exactly what happened, Brooke dying of septicaemia in April on Skyros without having seen action, Békássy a few months later in a hail of Russian bullets in Bukovina in June 1915.

Békássy's death was greatly mourned by his friends in England. Bedales Headmaster, J. H. Badley wrote warmly about him in the *Bedales Records*[56] and Frances Cornford composed a moving poem, (included in this volume) 'Féri Bekassy'(sic) written in 1915, a tribute mourning her young Hungarian friend.[57] Keynes was greatly shaken when he first heard of the death from Békássy's younger brother John, though Noel too had sent him a copy of the last letter. He wrote emotionally to Duncan Grant saying that Békássy "was certain to be killed" and "When one thinks of him, it is his goodness ... one seems to remember."[58] Duncan Grant told David Garnett, "He's the only person I had any real affection for, that has been killed so far."[59] One of the most moving tributes was written by

---

[54] Békássy to Noel. May 1915, first published in *The Hungarian Quarterly*, No.199 (Autumn 2010), p. 113.

[55] *Song of Love*, p. 278.

[56] Bedales Records 1914-1915.

[57] Frances Cornford, *Collected Poems*, London, 1954, p.50. Part of the poem is included in an essay by Helen Fowler in *Cambridge Women*, ed. Edward Shils and Carmen Blacker, CUP, Cambridge, 1996, pp.137-158.

[58] Keynes to Grant, 24 July 1915, Keynes, Vol III, BL, MS Add.57931, f.92. Also Keynes's letter to his mother 17 July, 1915, referred to by R.F. Harrod, *The Life of John Maynard Keynes*, Penguin Books, 1972, p. 237.

[59] Frances Spalding, *Duncan Grant*, Chatto & Windus, London 1997, p.175.

Gordon Luce[60] to Maynard Keynes from Burma (included in this volume).

When Peter Grant-Watson learnt of his friend's death, he contacted Békássy's mother Emma, sending her an unpublished English poem by her son.[61] Many years later in his autobiography, he describes Békássy as "a lovable and stimulating character, and with a great sense of humour and fun."[62] Frank Laurence (Peter) Lucas also remembered him as an unusual person who "had the gift for being outside and inside himself almost at the same time."[63]

It was John Maynard Keynes, who was instrumental in getting the memorial plaque to Ferenc Békássy erected in the chapel of King's College, of which Peter Jones writes in this volume. Keynes also supported the publication of a posthumous volume, *Adriatica and other poems*, a selection of Békássy's poems and aphorisms published by Leonard and Virginia Woolf's Hogarth Press in 1925.

Békássy's Hungarian writings were published by his family between 1915 and 1918, but he remained relatively unknown in his native land. With the publication in 2010 of *Békássy Ferenc egybegyűjtött írásai* (Ferenc Békássy's Collected Writings) a 455 page-long collection of Békássy's poems and essays, edited by Tibor Sennyey Weiner, a renaissance of interest in his work began. Sennyey Weiner is to be given credit for the research and determination with which he has championed Békássy's cause in Hungary, putting him on the literary map as one of the most talented poets of World War I. In 2013 Békássy's letters to Noel Olivier translated into the Hungarian by Virág Balogi[64]

---

[60] Gordon Luce, see Main Characters.
[61] *The Imago*, p. 236.
[62] *But to What Purpose*, p. 155.
[63] In his Preface to *Adriatica and other poems*, Hogarth Press, 1925.
[64] *Békássy Ferenc szerelmes levelei*, (Love Letters of Ferenc Békássy) ed. Gömöri György and Weiner Sennyey Tibor, Aranymadár Alapítvány, Budapest-Zsennye, 2013, p. 149.

were published in Hungary to great acclaim. It is hoped that this present volume of Ferenc Békássy's poems in English and a selection of his letters to his English friends, will bring him to the attention of a wider audience. It is meant as a tribute to a young man, tragic victim of World War I, an Anglo-Hungarian poet who loved both the country of his birth as well as the country to which he owed his education.

George Gömöri and Mari Gömöri

ADRIATICA

AND OTHER POEMS

FERENC BÉKÁSSY

With a Preface by F. L. Lucas

Published by
Leonard & Virginia Woolf at The Hogarth Press
52 Tavistock Square, London, W.C. 1
1925

The title page of the only published edition of Békássy's English poems

POEMS

Introduction to the Poems

Ferenc Békássy is one of the few twentieth century poets, Rainer Maria Rilke (who wrote mainly in German and less frequently in French) being another, who was at home writing poetry in more than one language. In Békássy's case as mentioned in the Introduction, he not only wrote alternately in English and Hungarian but wrote versions of the same poem in both languages.

His first efforts in English are parodies and exercises imitating the poetic styles of English poets of the past whom he admired. Two of these written in 1912 were sent to John Maynard Keynes. The first one, 'The Prophet to Zuleika' is the first poem in this volume. The second one, 'Trunk-things floating...' in a verse form imitating Robert Browning's 'A Toccata of Galuppi's' describes his journey from England back to Hungary. This we have included in the correspondence to Keynes. After it was published in the *New Hungarian Quarterly* in 1980, Patrick Leigh Fermor, one of Britain's great travel writers in his book *Between the Woods and the Water* (1986), says that 'this light hearted skit 'showed 'great promise'.

The language and the verse form of Békássy's more serious poems which include sonnets and elegies, resemble those of his contemporaries, known as the 'Georgians'. He favours rhyming couplets and quatrains and says in a note that his contemporaries cannot differentiate between short and long syllables in English versification. His themes are of nature, though described in verbal brushstrokes like an impressionistic painting, of longing, unrequited love and nostalgic references to antiquity. Not all of his poems in English survive, as he was highly self-critical and destroyed many, but those that do stand up to the scrutiny of time alongside those of his contemporaries. This in spite of the fact that at one point, when he was coming to the end of his Cambridge years he tells Noel, that 'my soul is filled with dust when I try to write [in English].'

'Adriatica', excerpts of which we include, is the only narrative poem which has survived. It is a story about a girl and three young men on a yacht-trip on the Adriatic Sea. The three male characters pursuing her are based on Noel Olivier's admirers, Herbert being Rupert Brooke and Adrian Stephen moulded into one, Philemon being James Strachey, and Anthony, Békássy himself. The girl Amrita, (nectar in Sanskrit) with her brown skin and long black hair represents Noel. The men are pursuing her but she rejects them calmly, refusing to believe in love. Békássy above all is a lyrical poet and he himself says that the best parts of 'Adriatica' 'have nothing to do with the story'. As he sent different versions of the poem to various friends including Noel, it is not known whether the one published posthumously in 1925 is the final version.

In his Hungarian poems Békássy appears far less inhibited, expressing his love for Noel, something only hinted at in the English poems. He experimented with different techniques following the modern poetic movement in Hungary using blank verse or unrhymed free verse, though the two poems included in this volume are in traditional verse form.

Rupert Brooke and Békássy both continued writing poetry after they joined up. Brooke's sequence of sonnets, '1914' written in October that year, has an air of bravura and exuberance about the outbreak of war and is about the sacrifice he personally will make on behalf of England. It begins with the lines:

'Now God be thanked Who has matched us in this hour,
And caught our youth, and wakened us from sleeping'

The last sonnet the famous 'If I should die…'uses the word 'England' or 'English' no less than six times.

Békássy's poem of the same title on the other hand is more universal. Though he says the young cavalryman, 'who fell without a murmur '[had gone] 'gaily, since go he must', the poem considers the war a tragedy transcending borders, and he stresses the individuality of each death. This elegy is about the futile death of all those young men killed, regardless of nationality, ending with the lines:

'Mourn, O my sisters! singly, for a hundred thousand dead.'

To the end of his life Békássy continued writing poetry in both languages. The last one he wrote in English was 'Into Thy Hands , O Love' in December 1914, in which imagining himself as an old man he is reminisces about Noel, mourning lost love.

POEMS WRITTEN
IN ENGLISH

The Prophet to Zuleika[1]

Hora novissima, tempora pessima sunt, vigilemus![2]

When, pleading passionate for feelings fashionèd deep
from the heart
I waited silently, hoping by love to see thy evry part
Raised to sublimity; (love scorns what limit he easily scapes,
Fashions reality tortured mentality drearily apes)

Wily with passionless wearying wariness, why did you cast
Dust of doubt over me, lo! who aspired to be first, who
    was last,
Ranked with the godhead high, raised voice to prophesy
    unto the lands?
Tamed it the beast of prey, ere night o'er takes the day,
    under your hands.

---

[1] The title is an allusion to Max Beerbohm's novel *Zuleika Dobson* (1911) which
satirises undergraduate life at Oxford.

[2] 'It is the last hour, the worst of times, let us be vigilant' first line of a poem ,
written by the 12th century monk, Bernard of Cluny, part of a long poem,
De Contemptu Mondi (Scorn for the World).

So must cries, passionate, clamorous, perforate ever
    the shame
Blameless virginity silently brings to me! Back whence
    he came,
Wild among beasts that rage, back to his heritage must
    the man roam
Brute who aspired to rise, whom you made fool -
    or wise? - Lust is his own!
Mute, mawkish, senseless, lewd, so shall he reap the fruit,
    since he has sown![3]

Sonnet

Do storms conspire to save the standing corn,
Or bees to fill the flowers with honey dew?
For pleasures come before desires are born
And joy, till every heart to heart is true!
Now, now, how intimate your world appears,
What fit endeavour for a sweeter prize:
Dewdrops, than misery's, are better tears;
Than Love, still waters have more sweet surprise.
No sorrow then was cause of your despair,
Bold lover! - Come: to leave the fancy free
Walk where the buoyant swallow cleaves the air
And pluck the apple from the apple tree.
All happiness be yours, all powers even,
Who find, than Love's delight, a better heaven.

---

[3] Békássy sent this poem to Maynard Keynes with the following footnote:
    'The rhymes are plainly stunning and the sense is there; I hardly think the
    metre[sic] of Bernard of Cluny exemplified here is really such a grand' mystère.'
    The poem appears to be an exercise in rhyme and meter.

The Adventurer

A Traveller's is the word
From unknown lands. 'There, soon,
Trooped past the magic herd
Before its shepherd Moon.

Across the firmament
Tall flames do walk in state.
Burning with vast intent
For ever there they wait.

An azure lake was spanned
By stones that built a way.
I left the magic land
Unvisited by day.

A field encompassed me,
Where many kingcups grow
By pools beneath a tree.
I thought of him I know

Whose thoughts with mine can be
Like lambs among the grass.
Joy sang there quietly:
I did not dare to pass.'

A Boat for Love

Give me but the boat, I say,
Sorrow never follows;
Fare you well! I shall not stay:
Winter's in the hollows.

Where the wastes stretch far away,
Blurred with rain and blending,
Or to-morrow or to-day
Love shall have an ending.

There the swans dash through the wave,
On the water swinging;
I shall make my scallop rave
With the tempest springing.

I shall come before the snow;
I shall come a-courting
To the hazy depths below
Shadows at their sporting.

When the snow before the rout
Drifts against my sail,
I shall turn my boat about
Straight across the gale!

Over endless waters wind,
Chase the fast stream faster;
All but love is left behind:
Death shall prove the master!

Now the sparrows cease their cry;
Silence stands appalling. -
Still and far and deep I'll lie,
Where the snow is falling.

Fragmentary Views

1. Water.

Larches all green and chestnuts hardly white,
Rough grass, and clumpy marigolds I see
Within the water; but how changed quite!
- A world begins, where tree doth grow from tree.

What dusky Earths, what Fires at all compare
With thee, what Air, what Shadows lightly wrought,
Thou living Water! Settled softly there,
Proud with the proud reality of Thought.

2. Clouds.

Yea, very swiftly do they veer, and fly;
Their shadow dapples the abundant vale,
And in a while no cloud is on the sky.
Their forms are fanciful, of texture frail:

And now like hounds in great pursuit they seem!
- Their prey will vanish in the opening morn.
Only a little while the trappings gleam,
And for a little space doth sound a horn.

3. Wind.

A-tiptoe up and down and all about
What folly prompts you, wind, from room to room?
Leave now the creaking staircases; go out;
Make sturdy movement all across the broom.

And in the heather-bells; or in a mead
Stiffen the hairs upon a horse's mane;
And, unreluctant as the moments speed
Soar to destruction in the slanting rain!

Alone Immortal

Here only once or twice the owlet calls,
Here the wind bloweth only for a space,
Joy cometh like a morning in this place,
But hope need never be, nor doubt at all.

Death only is quite certain, and his death,
These silent sessions shall not change again,
Pledged by the last long spasm of pain
That shook his body, empty now of breath.

Cold sheath, Love's broken urn!
This then was all
Now is your earth compounded into clay.
Friend! I begin to bury you this day:
Thoughts to you kindred crowd your funeral.

I shall not carry flowers to your grave,
Certain there is not more than earth beneath.
Your memory I shall not always save,
Nor of my sad thoughts make the useless wreath.

But when the flow of secret tears is spent,
Skies talk to me of you, stars say your praise,
A world is altered everywhere you went,
And men's ways, in some strange part, are your ways.

May 1913

The Last Fragment

Now deep midnight must cling to hills and spurs
In that far country where my friend and I
Once walked on earth together, and the firs
Will shake a little as the wind will die.
Each grain of sand must shift uneasily,
And hazy mists will come when no wind stirs
Over the heath. On such a night it seems
As though the country were a desert; men,
If any walk there, spirit-like; and dreams
Grow few, and spoken words uncanny then.
Forsaken roads there lie across the sand,
Pools curl beneath some over-knotty tree,
And curly clouds pass far above the land.
But that dim country woke no fantasy,
Conjured no judgement out of every mood.
I suffered there; so that I used to brood
Seeing with incomprehension something strange,
Till time and good remembrance worked a change.
The elements of Wonder lie beneath
The least or greatest object viewed but so.
Tall grasses socketed with haulm and sheath,
And bodies growing as the grasses grow;
Love that was love a thousand years ago...

Death's Love

Pale Death, still Death had taken him in his arms
When in the morning stillnesses he woke;
    But neither spoke.

Faint lying, careless even, he was still:
With longing looked the Other in his eyes
    Wherein a lulled surprise

Too quiet for love, although Death's silence played
About his limbs, Death's curls dropped round
    his head
      That drooped, half-wearied.

Amid the stars, God's treasure of pale stones,
A shadow now moves endlessly along,
    Travelling long and long.

Over the foam-clouds of the heaving air
Death seeks the love of one he holds too dear,
    Who, silent, will not care.

Adriatica[4]

(excerpts)

1.

How could lovers live more wisely
Than the way that lovers use?
Sport she early, late arise he,
Peace and ardour neither lose.

But though Romeo is happy
In his mistress' sheets and arms
Wind's his wisdom if mayhap he
Find she doth refuse her charms.

Solitary love! Ah! senseless
Lovers grow, denied their lust,
Foolish in their pained intenseness
When they sigh because they must.

They can never plead so brightly,
Stature, lip, and hand and eye –
But two words, disdaining lightly,
Madden, cloy and stultify.

Does she yield if he solicit?
Kiss without a thought of guile?
What the wisdom lies implicit
In his words and in her smile!

---

[4] 'Adriatica' Békássy's epic poem, giving the title to the posthumously
published volume.

But she keeps her cold aloofness;
Looks with kind unmoving eyes;
He is dumb and mad and useless;
She, who is not, seems more wise.

Friendship doth disarm the wooer,
Logic firm, persuasions fair;
Oh, the strongest vainly woo her
When she sits and plaits her hair!

2.

Now I am foolish; would you have me wise,
Let love return, to dwell within those eyes
Where now a stern determination rules,
'Love's inconvenient and lovers, fools'-
Love that alone its true purpose is
Lovers, who know what innocence is his.
    O do not seek to hoard for other years
What uncontrolled appears and disappears.
Refusing to remember, in that mood,
How happy lovers are, how love is good,
That moulds to destinies the formless clay.
Come, Love, before the time has passed away!
Your change, my ecstasy, may't not be far! -
Till when I foolish, but you wicked are.

Sonnet

I am that bondsman whom an earthly grace
Has to your whims unquestionably knit;
Love clamoured in my earliest embrace
That I should perfect and accomplish it.
Do not despise me: for the task is great;
I am not humbled in a lowly cause:
Love is no child, in ignorance elate,
Nor laughs and claps its hands without a cause
Come therefore; if my love be like the sea
And cannot its own ecstasy contain,
Be you my gentle wind and let me be
Your origin and virtue once again;
And tears and kisses be the fountain whence
Shall flow a new world's perfect innocence.

Asheham House,
24 April 1914[5]

---

[5] See letter to Noel 30th April 1914.

Hoc Erat in Votis[6]

All night I lay awake upon my bed
And every thought and limb was cramped with pain;
Bad memories beat their measure in my head,
And on the window of my room the rain.
Then I remembered, how one night we stood
In a fair garden full of solitude,
All friends, a bold and glamorous array,
The last time there to view the end of day.
It was a warm abundant day of spring,
And then the nightingales began to sing,
Each answering to each, and all the air
Was full of sudden melody; and there,
Where we had met, we parted, by those elms
And pools, and temperate Hesperian realms:
Fields were at even, when the birds are gone,
The water like a playing child talks on
In many characters, or vaguely sings
Without a tune, with many murmurings.
Sands by the swell of quiet sunny seas,
Where wandering birds alight to take their ease;
Shores where the surging wave invades the sand
And tears the rocks asunder, and the land
Suffers the sea, and crumbles in the change
That builds the new and makes the old things
strange.
Rocks where the confines of all ages are;
Where in their musing, for the wise, a star
Until the cycle of the years be full
Unaltered stands in sameness beautiful.

But now with troubled thoughts I think of you
Till the last moment and the last adieu,

---

[6]   'This was your vow', Latin.

When last I saw your face and lost you all,
Past sight; past not remembrance, not recall!
Here let this hour crown the bygone night:
I shall recall your presence, and the sight
Of those still walks, and gravel paths, and flowers
Entwined in trellis-work. The twilight hours
Pass quickly there: and there perhaps - who knows?
You walk still, where the thyme and heather grows:
The pleasant country where I cannot go;
And my emotion drags me to and fro,
Across waste desert countries, where the trees
Are few and desperate. You find your ease
In pleasant intercourse, where'er you be,
But chance and foolish fate have driven me
To range alone, and in strange beds at night
To turn and toss in pain. It is not light
To change so, so to wander, so to press
An idle quest, with helpless weariness;
To pass dim countries, dim and dull as they:
Therefore I think of somnolent Cathay
Of ice-bound Yukon, or the coloured South
Around the unaccounted Rio mouth,
The uncharted islands; or those nearer far,
Where Melada[7] and lone Lacroma[8] are,
Swathed in the star-bespattered Istrian night.

Thither, O come with me! In that still light
We'll make a pastoral journey, where the sea
Stands bathing in its own immensity.
O'er facts and scruples fancy shall prevail:
Over the stubborn waters we will sail
Often, as once I travelled; and attain
The calmness of the sleepy seas again.

---

[7] Island in the Adriatic Sea.
[8] Place-name in the Adriatic.

1914

He went without fears, went gaily, since go he must,
And drilled and sweated and sang, and rode in the
    heat and dust
Of the summer; his fellows were round him, as eager as he,
While over the world the gloomy days of the war
    dragged heavily.

He fell without a murmur in the noise of battle; found rest
'Midst the roar of hooves on the grass, a bullet struck
    through his breast.
Perhaps he drowsily lay; for him alone it was still,
And the blood ran out of his body, it had taken so little to kill.

So many thousand lay round him, it would need a poet, maybe,
Or a woman, or one of his kindred, to remember that none
    were as he;
It would need the mother he followed, or the girl he went beside
When he walked the paths of summer in the hush of his
    gladness and pride,

To know that he was not a unit, a pawn whose place can
    be filled;
Not blood, but the beautiful years of his coming life have
    been spilled,
The days that should have followed, a house and a
    home, maybe,
For a thousand may love and marry and nest, but so shall
    not he.

When the fires are alight in the meadow, the stars in the sky,
And the young moon drives its cattle, the clouds graze silently,
When the cowherds answer each other and their horns sound
    loud and clear,
A thousand will hear them, but he, who alone understood,
    will not hear.

His pale poor body is weak, his heart is still, and a dream
His longing, his hope, his sadness. He dies, his full years seem
Drooping palely around, they pass with his breath
Softly, as dreams have an end - it is not a violent death.

My days and the world's pass dully, our times are ill;
For men with labour are born, and men, without wishing it, kill.
Shadow and sunshine, twist a crown of thorns for my head!
Mourn, O my sisters! singly, for a hundred thousand dead.[9]

---

[9]   Written in English in Hungary, soon after the war broke out.

Into Thy Hands, O Love...

When I must die, a lonely man and grey,
And all my life lies open like a book,
Year after year close-written, I shall say:

How long is it, since I one day forsook
(Not yesterday! Long years and years ago)
My dearest of dear costly loves, and took

The uncertain journey all men had to go!
It was the time when men went out to war;
My way went north: I fought among the snow

Through sixty days of winter, while our star,
Our dreary little planet, rang again
With cries and wails and cannon. Now there are

No friends of mine who live; for some died then,
But some died afterwards. What matters it
-That was a bad war, but a time for *men*.

Though I had loved then, I was young: thought fit
Never to think of her, whose eyes were day
And starry night to me: she used to sit

With her hands clasped sometimes in such a way,
For many nights I dreamt of what must lie
Asleep behind her eyelids: meadows, gay

With purple crocuses, or daffodils,
Where she would wander with the winds, that fly
And drive the pearly rain across the hills.

Or yet a road perhaps, and such a sky
With fast grey clouds that skirt across the sun,
That she unhappy there perhaps would cry

Beside the reeds, where gurgling waters run.
- Now I am all alone, and well I know
That all my days and all my deeds are done,

It little matters that it happened so,
That - empty word to an on-speeding world -
She too is dead now many years ago.

I see the grains, that long ago have pearled
Through time's dim glass, and know them,
      tear by tear,
For vanity: but banner-like unfurled,

My love that was, is bright. My end is near.
Now all the rest is dust and emptiness.
I give myself to her - for she is here.[10]

Pápa, December 9, 1914

---

[10] Written in English in Hungary at his garrison

POEMS WRITTEN
IN HUNGARIAN

Translated by Owen Good

Amrita says:

But no, I never loved him! -true, I often marvelled
At his heart's embers flaring into light.
And if we parted ways, I parted weeping,
And it would make me smile when I'd discover
And read afresh some letters of his lines.

And how I loved those countless nights in winter!
If flames flared up occasionally in the hearth,
The russet light would soak his passionate body,
The blinking light of our shared words did glimmer
As they sought out plain, honest judgement both.

The things he'd ask - that my body burn in fever,
To rekindle the deep fire of his heart,
That passion might dictate itself to passion,
And drive my joy across a thousand dangers,
That lightning dash my cherished peace apart...

Oh! how cold...

Oh! how cold the autumn wind does feel...
And how thick the leaves of trees now fall!
How blood-filled the northern battlefield!

Tramping round the barracks summer last;
Chestnut trees were standing wan and pale:
Washed in dust by soldiers marching past.

Pale now too upon this autumn's day,
Now towards the blowing wind up North,
Off they go, here falling leaves, there death.

Here we've long since reaped our harvest yield;
When will reaping end there in the field?
Reapers! Soldiers! When will reaping end?[1]

(1914)

---

[1]   These two poems, in the original Hungarian, were published in Sennyey Weiner,
p. 148 and p. 47.

The four Olivier sisters, from left to right,
Margery, Bryn, Daphne, and Noel

LETTERS TO
NOEL OLIVIER

Noel Olivier (1892-1969)

Noel Olivier, the youngest of Sir Sydney Olivier's four daughters, was born on the 23rd of December 1892 hence the name Noel. She was of medium height, dark skinned and had long brown hair. According to Jaques Raverat her face was "very regular and unexpressive, even a bit hard". But he says that when she turned her large grey eyes on you, "One could hardly bear their gaze without feeling a kind of instant dizziness, like an electric shock". It was not only Rupert Brooke and Ferenc Békássy who fell under their spell, but James Strachey, with whom she also corresponded for many years and Virginia Woolf's brother Adrian Stephen, whose proposal of marriage she turned down. Her acquaintances say that though Noel was kind, she was reticent and unemotional. She had no intention of succumbing to any of her suitors: she remained rational, preferring not to marry early but to continue her studies and become a doctor.

Noel was the only one of the Olivier sisters to choose a discipline based on science and began to study medicine in

University College, London, qualifying in 1917. She married a colleague, Dr Arthur Richard, in 1920 and had five children, the oldest one, Ben being born in 1924. She became a well–respected paediatrician publishing one book, *Healthy Babies,* in 1935. She remained in touch with James Strachey with whom in the nineteen-thirties she had a long-lasting affair. As for Békássy, according to her daughter Angela Harris, years later Noel still often spoke warmly of her young Hungarian admirer.

Noel in 1909

Letter 1 – Easter Monday, April 1911

Kis Sennye, Rum, Vas vm.

Easter Monday, April 1911

Dear Noel,

I write under pretext of apologising for my unceremonious departure. And as this is not enough to fill up a letter, I continue.

You went to Lapthorne's I suppose, and had a huge time: Sylvia,[1] wrote me a letter re Chronicle[2] the other day, mentioning this as a coming event. I wish I were not so far from everything! Here I am again in a sort of amphibian condition: at Sennye[3] where there is nobody, and in open country; in town, where there also seems nobody worth anything, and where I'm gradually being civilised. As far as things intellectual go, its muster is the weakest possible. These are apparent only in scattered *Schloss*[4] and manor about the country. As for instance in the case of a distant relation of ours[5] a most extraordinary man, very highly artistic, still more aristocratic and an aesthetic looker-on at life, who is head and shoulders above everyone else (physically also, as it happens) and hasn't budged from his own private nirvana till quite lately. I think I've told you of him already. Just lately he gave two lectures to a very select and still more stupid audience, about Dürer,[6] and about the Venetian painters. They simply gaped the whole time. Well, of course

---

[1] Phyllis Lapthorn and Sylvia Mundy were both contemporaries of Békássy and Noel at Bedales. Sylvia Mundy went on to study music in Dresden.

[2] *Bedales Chronicle*, magazine of Bedales School, edited by the pupils.

[3] Sennye or Kis-Sennye, present day Zsennye, village in Vas County, Hungary, location of the Békássy family castle.

[4] Castle (German).

[5] Verebi Végh Gyula (1870-1951), Békássy's second cousin, art collector, painter, related to the Békássys on the side of his mother Angela Bezerédj . He owned Sibrik Castle in Bozsok. Director of the Museum of Applied Arts in Budapest from 1917 to 1934.

[6] Albrecht Dürer, (1471-1528) German painter.

they are gay enough, though as for humour, I have seen but little trace of it as yet. Of course there are many more 'galanteries', and carried on more freely than would be the case in England. (We being less swathed intellectually.) But the musical element is great, flourishing especially in the Army, which is also the home of Beauty helped by ingenious man. (Since only officers of higher rank - that is old - are usually married men)

Well, of course I don't suggest one should be sensible, or especially brilliant in wit, or talk about more interesting things: all that doesn't matter and I wouldn't mind the whole society nor the *jeunesse dorée*[7] - only there are too many like Hedvig's father in the *Beloved Vagabond*,[8] who did not have a dung heap in his backyard as peasants do, but hid it away underneath the parlour. *Nicht so arg*:[9] but that *is* the sort of thing.

Then there is Sennye and of course crowds of things to do. We often play tennis. So it is a tremendous relief when one gets a change, as today when two girl cousins of ours came over to see us. They live at B[uda]Pest except in the summer, and are very much in society. Being therefore just as absurd, but in a far finer way. And really one can enjoy oneself hugely even thus.

Coming home I found the works of several new poets and new poems of a very Sappho-like poetess,[10] and of the man[11] at the head of *our* literary post-impressionist movement, whom I knew before. But in this, probably his last volume, he has ceased writing about the 'bruises of kisses that bite'[12] and worse stuff of the kind, and so, since he does not any longer hide himself in uncouth expressions and affectations,

---

[7]   Golden youth (French).

[8]   Novel, later turned into a play by William John Locke (1863-1930).

[9]   not so bad (German).

[10] Probably referring to Renée Erdős (1879-1956) whose sexually explicit collection of poems entitled *Aranyveder* (Golden Bucket) was published in 1910.

[11] Hungarian poet, Endre Ady (1877-1919) whose *Új versek* (New Poems,) published in 1906 ushered in a new age in Hungarian literature.

[12] Reference to a love poem of Endre Ady, 'I am a Burning Wound'.

it is, I'm afraid, very easy to see that he has nothing to say. I'm gone mad on the Sapphonic poetess. Besides, I've read *Love's Coming of Age*[13] - at least, and it has of course greatly impressed me. All the more as Gotch[14] and I talked a lot of such things when I was up at Cambridge last term. He's simply lost himself in it. But I must say it came rather opportunely after the vision I told you of (the woman who is dead) - as something instead of that.

Of course we're doing lots of things here. First and foremost, we've got two horses and so can again ride, as we've not done at home for a long time. And besides, one of them, an English thoroughbred, is simply marvellous. I've never seen anything like her. Fairly small, bay, and with a fine head, its movements are smooth like those of a ship. She really seems to swim when going trotting at a long pace, and has a short canter that is quite unsurpassable. Unfortunately her mouth is very sensitive, and my hands are horribly heavy: I only hope I won't spoil her. I was expecting great things but really nothing like this. The other is good, of course, but can't be spoken of in the same breath with this one.

I myself like riding better than any other thing of the sort - though I'm not much good - but occasionally we go out to shoot wild geese; there are crowds of them. It is very exciting to wait for them after the other has fired: and it isn't at all an unequal contest. They *can* fly silently, too! - Of course all this is made more enjoyable still by the fact that the wood is so wonderful, and one can see so much (having to keep quite still). Also, it brings out the savage in one, especially in me, as I am emphatically an intellectual savage. It sums me up altogether though you, having seen nothing of my savage, won't believe it.

---

[13] Book by Edward Carpenter (1844-1929), a friend of John H. Badley, Headmaster of Bedales and frequent visitor to the school.

[14] John Hugo Gotch, see Main Characters.

We play bridge, too, nowadays: I'm beginning to learn it and like it; but I still make a fair number of howlers sometimes. But one gets *very* slack here, quite unable to attend to anything properly. We boat a fair amount of course (quasi canoes), and go to pay visits - as few as one can - and I am trying to do some very boring history. Yes, and we get up every morning, and go to bed at night, - almost every night - and have four meals a day, and so on and so forth. That's interesting. As also, 'what porridge had John Keats?'[15] But I thought I was going to write something more or less possible.

A year ago, I would have 'let loose my geniuses' reins,' and would 'Ride spirit like on misty seas:' written about

'The sky with its *scurrilous* mist,

(This was the word I missed)

And its (Blakeishly) hungry cloud

Dark, terrible, *luminous* shrouds…'[16]

Etc. etc.

[…]

But this is utter bosh. At any rate I can't help it: it's getting too late to keep entirely sane. But these sort of outbreaks do not last long.

'*Je siffle un air. Ou - - i. Mais pas jusqu'à la fin.*' So Rostand.[17] -

By the way, you know Peter's[18] idea of getting together all older Bedalian songs, and printing them in a special supplement to the Chronicle. […]

I suppose you are now swotting hard - or no longer? Commiseration or congratulation as is fitting in either case.

As for my writing - the dreadful badness of which I am only just beginning to appreciate - I'm in a terrible state, simply

---

[15] The last line of the poem 'Popularity' by Robert Browning (1812-1889).

[16] These four lines are Békássy's parody of his own verse.

[17] 'I breathe in the air. Yes. But not completely.'(French) Edmond Rostand (1868-1918) author of *Cyrano de Bergerac*, one of Békássy's favourite plays.

[18] 'Peter' is Elliot Logwood (Peter) Grant-Watson, see Main Characters.

longing to write pages and pages, and without a single idea. But I see that unless I stop soon I'll begin to quote, probably from the visions (the woman above mentioned): since you know only Bacchus[19] - which I did away with, and, foolishly enough, re-wrote (with unconscious variations of course). Therefore, I won't go on. I might have written something more sensible - or something funny in this letter; 'Yesterday we were out on the river' - and there followeth a description. But although I'm thoroughly sick of this letter, I won't repeat last summer's proceedings, so have it you must.

A good deal of this may be put down to the lateness of the hour and the impossible condition of my brain. Any rate, here endeth.

Your _____ (anything you like to say)
F. Békássy

---

[19] A long poem by Békássy written in 1909/10. The English MS was lost, a later Hungarian version written in 1915 was published in Tibor Sennyey Weiner, ed. *Békássy Ferenc egybegyűjtött írásai*, Aranymadár alapítvány-Irodalmi jelen, Budapest-Zsennye, 2010, pp.70-81.

Letter 2 – 23 August 1911

Kis Sennye, Rum, Vas vm.

[23 August 1911][1]

Dear Noel,

What an absurd ass I am, to say the least of it! Do you know, that since you left Bedales last April, you have been more in my thoughts than anyone or anything else?

Wherever I am and whatever I do, from writing poetry to flirting on various occasions, - I always suddenly begin thinking about you. And really, there is no one else I care to be with so much - or say talk ~~to~~ with - there is no one else I can talk with! And supposing I were to begin by extravagant compliments. I would not say lovely, lovable, enrapturing, *charming* (in a proper sense of the word), still less, ravishing: but sensible, sympathetic, 'possible' and so forth - you see what I'm driving at? And I have nothing to give, I *want*. I cling and cringe: - this is anything but the 'overflowing cup'. Oh, but I was wrong just now, - you *do* look sometimes like - well, when you're not looking at me, and not talking; a head-on-one-side business that makes me want to - I don't know! Do everything and nothing - makes me hold my breath. But that's a thing you share with - to say the least of it - a good many others. That's not why. Oh, but it's so impossible! I'm going to this wretched place [Cambridge] where nobody has anything but Ideas - how I hate Ideas! Not yours! Of course you've got to be interesting somehow - perhaps you can be [interesting] by now [..] without them, like a marvellous woman, hardly more than a girl[2] though married - whom I've just stayed with at Uckfield, not so far from you. I don't know.

---

[1] This was the letter which made Rupert Brooke jealous when Noel showed it to him at Clifford's Bridge, see Introduction.

[2] Not known to whom Békássy is referring.

You couldn't then that's a dead cert. Oh, if you'd hear the stuff we talk here, the way we behave, it's *sickening!* Here I am for instance with a cousin (distant) of mine[3] - , a girl of 19 whom I've known as long as I've known anyone, and thoroughly, and we always *did* like each other, and we can't get on because I don't choose to flirt with her. So now you see. And then I think of contrasts - and there you are. *Now* what I want to know is what good this damned and hopeless and ridiculous letter is going to - or could possibly be supposed to do. But if I only did things because they were some good or had some sense, I'd be somewhat different.

Well, I've taken a good long time to say something - i.e. that you are a marvellous person - perhaps a strange thing to say *to* anyone, when one means it: and that I want you.

Why on earth did I ever go to England, when it is so impossible for me not to come back home to these ridiculous and senseless people, and this tangle of western ideas and eastern senses! That's what I gain from it - I like a thousand sensible things in England, and cannot exist without 'the air you breath' - and have to tear myself away and bury my better half, to come back to this benighted land where no one is ever going to do anything - like a dog who runs with the wolves again, because of his blood, and who has nothing else in common with them. I don't mean now: three years to come yet: but what are three years to the rest? More opportunities of getting together needs I shall not be able to satisfy. And I'm already thinking of when I shall next see you - I always do, till the occasion nears - and always curse myself for doing so.

And I wrote this letter because I wanted to tell you and wanted someone to hear it - like a baby when it isn't pleased with something.

---

[3]   Not known to whom Békássy is referring.

[P.S.]

Dear Noel,

Please don't think the letter I send herewith is in any way normal. On second thoughts I came to the conclusion that a howling baby is not exactly a good model to go by. Still, I send it because it's a 'golden opportunity' of showing myself up a bit - and I think you ought to know.

There is no need to take it seriously: one can quite well get on without noticing such things - 'nothing matters but the unimportant'. Don't answer unless you want to - I'm not expecting an answer - and please forget as much of this as is embarrassing.

Yours very sincerely
F. Békássy

King's College, Cambridge, about 1906

Letter 3 – 25 November 1911

6 St. Edward's Passage, Cambridge
(or King's College)

Saturday, 25 November 1911

Dear Noel,

From the land of artistic ties, eternal tea-cakes, imperturbable Bedders[1] and Wilde[2] ideas posing as rational, greeting. I know you are in London, but ~~do~~ am not quite sure of your address - else you would have seen something of me when returning from a week-end at Bedales. Yes I too have dared the deed and gone down all alone, but though I had a fine time would not do it again. I am not going to gossip about it, you know more than I do. Probably; and a Golden Age usually advertises itself. Rather, about some here; I have just come from Moorsom's:[3] you would have been amused if you saw him. The classic remark that he and John (the King, not the Artist)[4] are the only two historical characters whom no one has ever tried to whitewash, is no longer apposite; not his reply, that he was white-washing himself. Buoyant and free from associations, he has attained to sudden popularity, is acquiring a taste for witty conversation, is known as a cynic, and has achieved greatness. But in the evening he sits and reads the records of his foolish youth[5] (accurately tabulated, with letters, *some of yours amongst them*[6] neatly affixed) and if I come in then, he reads them aloud to me, looking over his spectacles.

---

[1]   Bedmakers employed by Cambridge colleges.
[2]   Pun on Oscar Wilde's name referring to the homosexual scene ongoing in Cambridge.
[3]   Raisley Moorsom, see Main Characters.
[4]   A reference to the painter Augustus John (1878-1961).
[5]   Moorsom's diaries.
[6]   '*yours among them*' is written upside down at the top of the letter.

I on the other hand, have greatness ~~forced~~ thrust upon me.[7] This entails, on the one hand acquaintance with the men of daffodil sock and smarmed-down longish hair; on the other, clever men who, under cover of Search for Truth, assume all poses in deep seriousness; and finally Rupert Brooke. From whom a note, just now, complaining of how terrible it is, in the words of Jesus Christ, to be without a domicile; asking me to a late breakfast, with kind advice to read Paradise Lost[8] (our favourite point of disagreement) tonight, so as to wake up late; if getting there before him, to go on reading it. But perhaps you know him.

I shall not enumerate more new acquaintances; they're all intellectual, very grand and 'select' - too much so! —But my reputation went before me, and the gates lifted up their heads.

Of Bedalians of interest to you, nought: though I saw Gotch today- deep in work, almost as much as Tusky[9] is and even Alix[10] at the 'Heretics'.[11] Heretics! I don't understand how they can call themselves that! The lecturer tonight, after explaining errors of Xtian[Christian] morality, went on to say, we agnostics must formulate—crystallise, he said! —our morality: then we can impose it. Having thus laid down the lines for the <u>new religion</u> he sat down: in the discussion, these Heretics tacitly assumed he was right in imposing it, and talked of ways and means. I thought it was tragic, registered a remonstrance , and went: I ought to have stayed to see the similarity between these

---

[7]   'Some are born great. Some achieve greatness and some have greatness thrust upon them', Malvolio in *Twelfth Night*, William Shakespeare. Act II. Sc. 5.

[8]   John Milton (1608-1674) *Paradise Lost*, 1667.

[9]   M.S. 'Tusky' Pease, after Bedales studied agriculture in Cambridge.

[10] Alix Sargant-Florence (1892-1973), after Bedales studied in Cambridge, married James Strachey in 1920 analysed by Sigmund Freud, while on their honeymoon in Vienna.

[11] Heretic Society, discussion group in Cambridge, founded in 1909 by C.K. Ogden. John Maynard Keynes, Bertrand Russell and George Bernard Shaw were all associated with it.

Heretics and Chesterton,[12] and to laugh.

Last summer I cycled through Limpsfield[13] (almost) with John Fothergill,[14] of Slade repute: too disreputable to look in. I spent a marvellous week with them. [Fothergills]

I've seen Peter Watson seen Justin,[15] seen the Arányis;[16] met Mr. Cornford[17] - and everyone of note, as I said. (My life has been a continual blending of Lunches into Teas and Teas into Coffees after Hall)[18] Do you know Mrs. Cornford? ~~Authoress~~ Poetess, thus

'Fat white woman whom nobody loves
Why do you walk through the field in gloves?'
Isn't it great?[19]

I shall be in London after term ends (with [Grant] Watson!) may I any time come down to L[imps]field to see you? If so, when.

It is getting late and I have not yet read Paradise Lost. So I must stop. I have seen (~~many~~ some) plays and things and am resolved to see the Russian Ballet[20] this term before I die.

Yours
F. Békássy

---

12 G.K. Chesterton (1874-1936) author, poet, lay-theologian, best known for his *Father Brown* detective stories. Other works include *Robert Browning*, 1903.

13 Home of the Olivier family.

14 John Fothergill, taught art at Slade Art School, author of *The Principles of Teaching, Drawing and the Slade School*,1907.

15 Justin Brooke, see Main Characters.

16 Jelly d'Arányi (1893-1966) and her sister Adila were a renowned Hungarian violin duo, who often performed in London. Many famous composers dedicated works to them. These include Ravel's (*Tzigane*), Gustav Holst's (*Concerto for two Violins*) and Bartók's fiendishly difficult 1st and 2nd Violin Sonatas.

17 Francis and Frances Cornford, See Main Characters.

18 Hall, short for Dining Hall in Cambridge Colleges.

19 Lines from Frances Cornford's poem 'To a Fat Lady seen from a Train' *Poems*, 1910.

20 Serge Diaghilev's ballet company Ballets Russes starring Nijinsky first performed in London in the summer of 1911 to enormous success. Diaghilev worked with the greatest artists of his time; painters Picasso and Bakst, the choreographer Michel Fokine and composers such as Stravinsky.

Letter 4 – 28 November 1911

King's College

Tuesday, 28 November 1911

Dear Noel,

!!! Letters crossing: theme whereon dull people make platitudes I simply jumped when I got yours. But I must explain. I said at the time I didn't think you'd answer my August letter.[1] I wasn't expecting an answer:[2] these things are usually so awkward (one day I'll write a novel to show how awkward they are) so, not knowing what you mightn't think of me for it, I had to write my last [letter] - a fair example of my sophisticated Cambridge state of mind - as though I had forgotten the other altogether.

You can't imagine how glad I am you weren't annoyed and accepted the flattery - *cum grano salis*, as I see. I didn't pine away in anxious expectation of an answer.

'And I shall die, I fear…

-Within a thousand year'[3]

expresses my then state of mind very well.

So you're coming on Saturday - to tea with whom? Anyone I know or am likely to know? If so can you invite me, or would I be a nuisance? At any rate I can 'hurry by' in K.P.[4] any time you like to say - if you say it exactly - on Saturday.

---

[1]   See Letter of 23 August 1911.
[2]   Noel's answer to the above letter must have been seen by Brooke, presumably at the breakfast mentioned, as the following day he writes to Noel from Kings Cross Station waiting room after having met her in London: 'I told you I hated Békássy when I saw your letter to him (not as much as I hated you, and me) I did not through 'jealousy'[…..] but because you wanted to see him more than you wanted to see me.(I thought.) You liked him more.' *Song of Love*, p.138.
[3]   Paraphrasing a speech of Cassius from *Julius Caesar* by William Shakespeare.
[4]   King's Parade, Cambridge, around the corner from St. Edward's Passage, where Békássy had his rooms.

Damn the *Zauberflöte!*[5] I can't go on Sat. Am I going to see anything of you on Sunday? Is there anything to prevent your coming to tea with me, and bringing some people you know, or perhaps Rupert can come?[6]

These can be dealt with later. At any rate write and tell me something definitely.

I am not going to curse away your 'worst weakness': it isn't; it's your worst disability. (*vide* Peter Watson whom people like because he is never thinks of liking to be liked). This is Shavian - or would be, were it a good neat epigram; so you can excuse the impertinence if you like.

I can't get over the fact that my August letter was terrible, but then all real things are. That's why a sophisticated attitude based pretending to be based on the truth, (thus evolving Cambridge intellectualism) it's a contagious disease quite irresistible. Rupert is, now, amazing - all the more because it doesn't strike one that he is. But what he must have been as the West Wind that drives all the leaves before it (cf. Slade Dance, or Shelley's *Ode to the W.W.*)[7] I hardly dare imagine.

Then, what say you of seeing me about in Cambridge - yes, everybody looks modestly important; but supercilious?! Hush! That is heresy, blasphemy! A confounding of Oxford

5   The Magic Flute, opera by Wolfgang Amadeus Mozart(1756-1791). The first English language production was performed in Cambridge on 1st, 2nd and 3rd of December in 1911 by the Cambridge Operatic Society at the now defunct New Theatre in St. Andrew's Street. It was translated by Edward Dent, Fellow of King's College, Cambridge, Professor of Music (1926-1941).

6   Brooke played a minor part in the production; that is probably why Noel came for the weekend. She arranged to see him for tea on Sunday afternoon and wrote 'I'm not bringing Békássy.' *Ibid.* p.140.

7   The theme of that year's Slade Art School fancy dress ball was the winds and leaves of 'Ode to the West Wind', a poem by Percy Bysshe Shelley (1792-1822). Rupert Brooke went dressed as the West Wind, in the costume he had worn in the 1908 Cambridge Marlowe Society production of *Comus*. Nigel Jones *Rupert Brooke, Life, Death & Myth*, 1999, p.116.

and Cambridge! The unpardonable sin! Are not <u>we</u> the earnest, the seekers after Truth?!

But I'm not quite Cambridgified yet - thank heavens!

Yours
F. Békássy
Write as soon as poss. —

Letter 5 – 1 December 1911 (Summary)

In this letter sent from Cambridge dated 1 December 1911, Békássy tells Noel which train to catch and agrees with her that being among 'intellectuals' will do her good.

Letter 6 – 25 December 1911

c/o J. Brooke esq.,
Leylands, Wooton
Nr. Dorking
[25 December] 1911
Xmas day, (of all absurdities!)

Dear Noel

Everybody is reading in different corners of various rooms, and I've just been doing so but Hilda Lessways[1] annoyed me so I came away. You know of course I'm staying with the Brookes[2] - a handful of brothers and sisters, Mr Hooper[3] and an old lady, parents being away. Xmas not worth describing, *vide* Irving,[4] everybody pretending to pretend his sort of thing.

The day after tomorrow, Lulworth,[5] Rupert, Catherine Cox,[6] Maynard[7] and people - and just about time too! Have you ever had other people's woes poured down your neck wherever you go?

With Justin we began by arguing about large and vague subjects but are spending our time better now by discussing how in Marlowe's time they [would have] pronounced 'Pythagoras,

---

[1] Novel by Arnold Bennett (1867-1931) English novelist.
[2] Justin Brooke's family, where Békássy is spending Christmas.
[3] Unidentified person.
[4] Washington Irving (1783-1859) American writer and historian, author of *A History of New York*,1809, in which he pours scorn on the legend of Santa Claus.
[5] Lulworth, Dorset, where one of their regular reading parties organised by Rupert Brooke took place.
[6] Catherine 'Ka' Cox (1887-1938) Newnham College, Cambridge 1910. Rupert Brooke's friend, later lover, married William Arnold-Forster in 1919.
[7] John Maynard Keynes, see Main Characters.

metempsychosis [8] (to scan a line of his) or what the famous passage in Hamlet

'the dram of eale

Doth all the noble substance of a doubt

To his own scandal'[9]

means; believe me, a most profitable discussion. (Do you remember the part in *The Egoist*[10] where the professor talks scholarly inanities with the man Clara eventually marries - I've forgotten his name)

And all the time I want to simply shriek (splitting the infinitive in justification of a standpoint I adopted against Justin - in a recent argument). Of course, really, that's a very nice position to be in.

Cambridge is a little anthill. That's why everyone there is so ridiculously serious (myself included, please!) i.e. we met Dickinson[11] today, who is staying with Bob Trevelyan the poet,[12] whose acquaintance I've made. Are you making anything of this letter? I think in parts it tries for style, but that's only because of Arnold Bennett (!!) - otherwise it's only a little strange. (But this is after no meal).

[...]

Unless I cease I shall degenerate to - I mean this letter will degenerate to a discussion of people's characters: or a dull discourse on my plans (or anyone else's), or a regulated attempt at a shriek. Therefore adieu!

Yours

F. Békássy

[...]

---

[8]   Quote from *Doctor Faustus*, play by Christopher Marlowe (1564-1593).

[9]   Quote From *Hamlet*, Act I. Scene 4. William Shakespeare (1564-1616).

[10] *The Egoist*, novel by George Meredith (1828-1909).

[11] Goldsworthy Lowes Dickinson, see Main Characters.

[12] Robert C. Trevelyan, a Cambridge graduate and a member of the Apostles, whose poems were included in the anthology *Georgian Poetry*, 1912.

Letter 7 – 17 January 1912

The Union Society
Cambridge

17 January 1912

Dear Noel,

-No answer and still no answer! What slackness! Or has my letter never got there?

You didn't miss much by not coming down to Lulworth; we did very little worth doing: everybody was old-serious and then Rupert broke down. I suppose you've heard.[1] He's in southern France now. Somebody always gets ill at these Lulworth parties - last time it was Jacques[2]. By the way, I saw a review of Rupert's poems, something to this effect 'the choriambics... are the best that have ever been produced in the English language - I say this having in mind Swinburne's[3] experiment on the subject'.

I wonder who wrote it: I don't think Rupert, who ~~must~~ sees they haven't always come off, will enjoy this.

Do you know the Thomases?[4] Mr. T. is marvellous. I saw a good deal of him while staying at the Jarrys[5] (last few days) Talked poetry of course: apart from the fact that he liked mine,

---

[1] Brooke had in fact written to Noel on 6 January 1912 to say he had been ill and was off to the South of France to recuperate. *Song of Love* p. 154.

[2] 'Jaques', Jacques Raverat, see Main Characters.

[3] Algernon Charles Swinburne (1837-1909) English poet and playwright. His best known collection of poetry is *Poems and Ballads*,1866.

[4] Edward and his wife Helen Thomas (who taught at Bedales) lived at Steep, near Petersfield. Edward Thomas (1878-1917) wrote mostly book-reviews until 1914 when encouraged by Robert Frost he began to write poetry. During his lifetime, the only book of verse by him was published under the pseudonym Edward Eastaway.

[5] 'Jarrys' the Jarintzoffs who lived in Petersfield and with whom Békássy often spent part of his holidays. The son Dimitri Jarintzoff was a fellow-pupil at Bedales. His mother, Mrs. Nadine (Nadiezhda Alexeyevna) Jarintzoff translated from the Russian and in 1914, published a book *Russia: The Country of Extremes*. Jerome K. Jerome mentions having stayed with the family in Russia in his autobiography *My Life and Times*, 1926, p.190.

he's tremendously sound. Most people are merely brilliant - if they're anything.

I've been talking bosh since 5 pm yesterday, with intervals for sleeping. The cause, as usual, the root of all evil, is Bliss.[6] You met him at my rooms. Isn't he perfectly magnificent? (I merely <u>forgot</u> to ask this earlier)

I've hardly seen anyone else except uncle Raisley - newly <u>christened</u> Satan, it shows the pose he's at present adopting - I've never seen such a sophisticated sentimentalist. It's quite a joy to see him adopting superior attitudes before another Kingsman Felkin,[7] [...] who's also a sentimentalist but 'uncooked' and unsophisticated. Yet they know about his diary! Justin Brooke said he would like to get *The Comedy of Errors* up as an OB play.[8] He was complaining of people who refuse to act. I came up with Paully[9] and a popgun fiddle with which he was girt about. i.e. he's going to the Isle of Montebello - Australasia; hence he is practicing the use of his weapons. The gun is offensive, but the violin is to be his *pièce de résistance*.

Tonika[10] wrote to me lately to say my last letter to her was <u>absurd</u> and <u>silly</u>. Can you understand and sympathise? (Of course she had more to ~~wade~~ - get through - 8 pages!)

[...].
Yours
F. Békássy

---

[6]   Frank Bliss, see Main Characters.

[7]   Arthur Elliot Felkin (1892-1968) student at King's, close friend of Raisley Moorsom.

[8]   OB: Old Bedalian.

[9]   Paul (Pauly) Montague, zoologist and instrument maker, Bedalian.

[10]   Antonia Békássy, see Main Characters.

Letter 8 – 10 February 1912

King's College

Saturday, 10 February 1912

Dear Noel,

Well, Lulworth may be a place of torment 'where their worm dieth not'[1] (though their fire *was* quenched) but the Dorset rocks are good! And at any rate we pretended to do things there: not so in Cambridge: here one talks so much that one can do nothing. I should like - for that very reason - to write a Decameron[2] of the place: - I wonder why no one has done so about either[3] university ; people write Zuleika Dobsons[4] and like absurdities, but when they're given some really decent material, they simply don't take any notice! I may do it some day: till then, if I go on having inane ideas like this I shall have to publish a leaflet of 'Themes.' (all rights reserved) Though there is a disadvantage: *we* don't, here, do the marvellous things you describe, the dancing and the New Year's Eve: James[5] *was* up here, it is true; but I find no record of his having worn any sort of drapery; Warwick[6] was up too, I suppose - but *tempora mutantur, etc.*

Or by misquotation, *tempora mutantur <u>nec</u> nos mutamur in illis*[7] - shall never grew wings - in a way much more true than the actual saying. And certainly much more of a pity!

I shall imagine your dancings - it does one good after this

---

[1] Quotation from the Bible: Mark 9:47-48.

[2] Reference to the collection of tales, *The Decameron* by Giovanni Boccaccio, (c.1313-1375).

[3] [FB note] pardon the imparalleled conceit of this word!

[4] Max Beerbohm's humorous novel, with the subtitle "an Oxford love story", published in 1911.

[5] James Strachey, see Main Characters.

[6] Richard Turner-Warwick, pupil at Bedales school in 1911-12.

[7] By adding the word 'nec' Békássy alters this Latin axiom to its opposite meaning that is, "times are changing, we are *not* changing with the times".

sort of atmosphere! I do really and truly believe there are *crowds* of people here who, if asked

'Who fished the murex up?

What porridge had John Keats.'[8]

Would (without reference to text) solemnly and seriously expound! - But of course this is bosh: I like it all *immensely*, and after all, the questions above are very good bases for an argument. 'How pleasant is divine philosophy' - as long as it treats of porridge and the like! My Decameron, companions - how I wish they existed!

At present we are two in number, - you've met the other man in my room, Bliss, - and unless we are possessed by Devils (whose name is legion) we ~~can~~ are too few. I was startled at your casual mention of a book I don't know, and you having read tomes and tomes of it (so it seems) and still 'palpitating' to get on! What is it?

But read André Gide - *Prométhée*, or *Nourritures Terrestres*, or *Le Roi Gandaule* (a play) - he is the most marvellous man in existence, he is the most tremendous and great and amusing and absurd: he is the only continental writer there has ever been who is *humorous* (I don't mean witty). Or don't you think this is humorous:

'C'est une livre que mangea Jean[9] à Patmos

Comme un rat - mais moi j'aime mieux les framboises.

Ca lui a rempli d'amertume les entrailles,

Et après, il a eu beaucoup de visions.'[10]

Prométhée is easy French. He is the *only* man who really feels and manages to live by feeling. Imagine sitting in the open window of a train all night, to feel how the movements in the air touch one's shut eyelids! Imagine writing a whole part of a book just about gardens and fruits, without a single thought or a thing that

---

[8]   The last two lines of Browning's poem 'Popularity'.

[9]   [FB note] the supposed writer of Revelations [sic].

[10] Quotation from the poem 'Ronde' from André Gide's (1869-1951) *Les Nourritures terrestres* (1897).

happened, and not being boring! But I forgot: you may not think much of this sort of thing. I have not read anything much but Gide - I couldn't read anything else - I can't even read him for long, I am so full of things. I am going in a while to Maynard's rooms, lots of people will be there - I want to talk a tremendous lot. [...]

I was in town on Sunday - waiting for a train to Petersfield (but, only went on business and came back next morning) and so went to see the Jaques' - the only address I knew. By the way, the Gides are mostly a result of this. [...]

You know I suppose that Justin is already in Moscow, seeing Mr Gordon Craig's[11] productions and doing I can't guess what else. Everything, perhaps, except writing.

I am in a very inane condition altogether. I do not work (I know I shall try to make up for it by overworking for a week some time and making myself entirely miserable), spending most of the day doing little if anything - with Bliss - who is a perfectly marvellous person, beyond anything imaginable.

Oh, and playing fives, too, occasionally: as a reaction. I like it quite immensely and after I have got a 3rd class in the First Part of my Tripos I shall turn athlete. I am quite intractable by reason, do absurd things in a casual way, and write gibberish - a thing I've never done before. Real gibberish, in verse. About stars shooting out towards you like snails' eyes: but mostly about unknown and quite meaningless things in made-up words.

I wish I read the Masefield poem.[12] I think I shall, before I go write any more. It's late anyhow. I don't know when I can continue, there is a pathetic canoe waiting for me *miles* down the river - I must get it tomorrow morning (Insert appropriate sentiments - I think the Cam is *very* beautiful when one has to

---

[11] Edward Gordon Craig (1872-1966) co-directed *Hamlet* with Stanislavsky during the 1911/12 season in the Moscow Art Theatre.

[12] Noel must have quoted John Masefield(1878-1967) in her previous letter to Békássy.

paddle a wretched thing up it for hours and hours and hours!

Monday. I had too much to do yesterday. As a matter of fact we enjoyed paddling the canoe up very much - it was such a grand day, with all colours twice as bright as usual: (Again insert appropriate sentiments) I don't think, after all, that my Decameron is a good idea: yesterday a lot of us made ourselves (or each other) quite mad by discussing what were Universals - of course we couldn't get anywhere. And this morning I was doing some work and found that Thomian and post-Thomian Scholiasts,[13] a few (650) years ago also discussed the same, went mad about it and could get to no conclusions.

And how can one write anything readable about a discussion of this sort? And the whole place is full of them. E.g. I am just beginning to read for a paper I shall give on 'The Renaissance and the Reformation' - I have great ideas about the relation between them, everyone writes utter bosh about it. But it's not *amusing*!

I am going to lunch with 'Mac' (Macaulay) the K[in]gs tutor[14] - you may have heard of him. It will be very funny, he is *so* shy, and somehow when I get there I never know which leg to stand on either.

I'm looking forward to a tramp across ~~of~~ to Petersfield at the end of term - to be accomplished in true Borrovian[15] style. It would be rather fun to copy his talk on the way! Well, I shall have to ~~go~~ stop and prepare for the coming ordeal of a lunch - Salve nos, Domine -[16]

Yours

F. Békássy

---

[13] Békássy refers here to the scholastic philosophy of St Thomas Aquinas (c.1225-1274).

[14] William Herrick Macaulay (1853-1936) mathematician, Fellow, Senior Tutor in 1912 and later Vice-Provost of King's College, Cambridge.

[15] 'Borrovian' is a reference to the novel *Romany Rye* (1857) by George Borrow (1803-1881). Edward Thomas (see Letter 7, footnote 4), published a biography of George Borrow in 1912 and may have recommended the novel to Békássy.

[16] Lord Save Us.

Letter 9 – 5 April 1912

Kis Sennye, Rum, Vas vm.

5 April 1912

Dear Noel,

You must excuse me for not writing before - but of course, I forgot, I *did* see you at the end of term. I went on to Bedales, found Eva[1] had gone to the Turners at Ryde and stayed for a few days enjoying myself. Neither Phyllis nor Pump[2] were there. It seems everyone who wants to learn something goes away from school for a few weeks! Dorothy[3] was very upset - or rather, in a funk, about Hugo[4] - I wonder if you've heard from her. I have a sort of idea Hugo never went there after all. Everything else was very grand. My brother (now a prefect)[5] and Zilliacus[6] were liquefying gases, one could tell from the Biol.Lab. by the fumes. If prize-work comps interest you, you've seen results in the *Chronicle*. The drill was very good. I tried to practise with them one afternoon but they are quite beyond me. Maynard Keynes has written from Monte Carlo, where, with Gerald,[7] he is gambling hard, and so I know about Rupert.[8]

---

[1] Éva Békássy, see Main Characters.

[2] 'Pump'- nickname of unidentified person.

[3] Dorothy Winser at Bedales School from 1910 to 1915. Later wife of Josiah Wedgewood.

[4] Hugo Trzebicki, at Bedales from 1906 to 1910, who made a career as a chemist in Poland. Hugo Trzebicki was expelled from Bedales in 1910 over a hushed up attempted suicide, having been involved with the above named pupil, Dorothy Winser. In one of his notebooks, Békássy writes in Hungarian, that in 1910 a friend of his, 'H', took poison but recovered and left Bedales.

[5] István Békássy, see Main Characters.

[6] Konni Zilliacus (1894-1967) writer and British politician. At Bedales from 1909 -1912.

[7] Gerald Frank Shove (1887-1947), economist, Fellow of King's College, Cambridge.

[8] Rupert Brooke, who had suffered a nervous breakdown in January at one of their camps, was in the South of France with his mother and subsequently travelled to Munich with his then girlfriend Ka Cox. Nigel Jones, *Rupert Brooke, Life, Death, Myth*, pp. 216-218.

I am become quite Hungarian again. I have three deep vertical lines between my eyebrows and my lips are expressively curled. Besides which, it does seem quite absurd that I should write in English and know about English things as though I were English myself. It is very obvious that I shall have to come home as soon as possible. I don't in the least want to go back to Cambridge; it is quite useless for me to do so: I might just as well stay here, manage some land, talk politics and keep bees.

Till lately I have been in town, it was very exciting while the crisis lasted. I got to know all sorts of things one doesn't read in papers. I also went about a bit but the people are atrocious; they were all gloating over a wretched affair and you could see their faces lighting up whenever the topic was approached. I debauched a little but Szhely[9] is a dull provincial town.

After this government resigns - it can only hold on a few years at the most - the whole country will be smothered in clericalism: all *my* generation are intensely clerical. It is a fine prospect for us! Already at the Budapest university there are only two parties, to one of which one must belong: Clerical or Philo-Jew. There are fixed party opinions on all matters of learning. Justin, I hear, is back - or just about to arrive - have you heard from him? How is he?

For the last three days I have been quite alone in the house. All the rooms uninhabited since Xmas; camphor and spiders and dust. Outside rain and a cold north wind. Last night it *froze* and at B[uda]pest there has been snow! The cherry trees are just flowering and the grass is covered with violets, anemones, wild hyacinths, etc.

We went for a ride in town, Tonika, myself, and a whole lot of others. We were very wild and it was quite good fun.

---

[9]   'Szhely', abbreviation of Szombathely, town in Western Hungary.

There has been rain this year: but once this wind stops
~~the~~ it will be perpetually fine, perhaps even hot, and of course
everything will remain very fresh, and the meadows damp and
a little swampy. What a business moving into a place is! Even
when it is half furnished. The cart with the furniture had quite
an adventure, breaking down in the evening, some distance
from anywhere.

I have made a great discovery: - found the journals of an
ancestor of mine, a young lady in 1820,[10] in MS in the Library.
It is written in French. She was a very fine person, you can
imagine the type - in Biedermayer[11] - very exquisite etc. Half is
before, half some years after she married. She is well known, as
she wrote a book of short rhymes on which our grandmothers
and even our mothers were all brought up. My sisters, too.
Something like the *Child's Garden of Verses*.[12]

I shall try and see something of Sylvia on my way back,
through Dresden.

Yours
F. Békássy

---

[10] Amália Bezerédj (1804-1837) author of the first (illustrated) Hungarian book for
children: *Flóri könyve* (The Book of Florie,1839). Her diary which Ferenc Békássy
mentions reading in manuscript was destroyed during World War II.

[11] Correct spelling Biedermeier, early 19th century style popular in Germany and
Austria and Hungary.

[12] Popular children's book by Robert Louis Stevenson (1850-1894).

Letter 10 – 5 May 1912

K.C.C

A.D [5 May] 1912

Dear Noel,

I hope you won't be bored by this, but I am sick of work and don't want to hear people talk bosh and so can't help writing. I suppose you have heard from Dorothy lately; I got a letter from Hugo a while ago - from what I gather, Bedales authorities have been unspeakably and quite needlessly absurd[1] - but it's no use writing about this. I hope Dorothy *is* going back to Bedales and will come up to Cambridge. I am of course *very* disappointed that Hugo won't - you can imagine how I was looking forward to having him here! -

I can't express how utterly tired I am of everything: quite indifferent to my own and anyone else's feelings or circumstances: quite tired of thinking about anything at all, still more of talking. I don't mean I am despondent.

It is, I suppose, the price one pays for excessive activity and agitation at some time.

I think I had better write down a few facts. I missed Sylvia at Dresden, in some mysterious way; but she writes she will be back in June and up here for May week, so I suppose I shall see her.

Justin is at Bad Kissingen, Bohemia,[2] recovering; I never realised how serious a relapse he had at Naples, but anyhow he is quite fairly well now - well enough to laugh at Bohemian ways, and consider himself and a few others the only people worth considering. Among the 'few others' are the Cornfords: and I agree with him in including them, but most Cambridge people don't seem to. It is very puzzling, I can't make out why people like Shove or even Lytton[3] shouldn't. The other night I went to see

---

[1]   For Dorothy and Hugo's relationship see Letter 9, footnotes 3 and 4.
[2]   Bad Kissingen is in Bavaria, not as Békássy states in 'Bohemia'.
[3]   Lytton Strachey, see Main Characters.

them and found Cornford alone - I was very frightened because he talks too little usually, and is so reserved; I thought it would be agony for both of us: but I think we were both quite pleased with the result. Though we talked for three hours.

At last I shall see Maynard ride - we are going out this afternoon. I am very glad, because I miss it (riding) so much here.

Norton[4] and Lytton are up; but crowds of people seem to be going away to the most distant corners of the world. It is rather unfortunate that all the people I care about here are quite ancient - except, of course, Bliss - but then one sees so little of him, he has a lot of friends I hardly know. - My Mays[exams] are in a month's time, but as I have no scholarship (which they would take away after it) I don't care how I do. But I have hardly worked at all till this term. And now there are such opportunities of lying in punts etc -

[...]

Don't you think it is absurd that people should go off to Rangoon or to Clifton and never be heard of again?[5] (I don't think you know them, but that makes it no better)

I don't know if you've heard of the Austrian[6] who is here; he is 20 and last term, after much deliberation, decided not to go in for aeronautics and to take moral sciences here? He now utterly confounds Russell and Moore;[7] the latter says he can't understand his arguments, but sees by the way in which

---

[4] Henry Norton, mathematician at Trinity College, Cambridge, member of The Apostles.

[5] This refers to Gordon Luce, see Main Characters.

[6] The 'Austrian' is Ludwig Wittgenstein (1889-1951) Austrian philosopher, member of Trinity College, Cambridge. Elected to the Apostles in 1912. During World War I. volunteered for the Austro-Hungarian army. Author of *Tractatus Logico-Philosophicus* (1922). Settled in Cambridge, England in 1929.

[7] Bertrand Russell (1872-1970) philosopher and political writer. Fellow of Trinity College, Cambridge. Wittgenstein's friend, he wrote the English introduction to *Tractatus*. George Edward Moore (1873-1958) philosopher, author of the influential *Principia Ethica* (1903). Member of the Apostles, becoming Professor of Philosophy at Cambridge after World War I.

they are spoken that they are true! Norton has seen him and is quite gone on - his intellect.

I wish Rupert[8] were here, I haven't seen him for such a long time. I don't even know whether he is in Germany again or has again come back. (Later) People are just getting back to Bedales. I wonder if my brothers are there.

I have been reading an MS[9] I found at home, of the journal of one of my Great-Grandmothers, famous for nursery rhymes, she made later. At the time she writes she was about 21; halfway through the MS she gets married. [...] She is very marvellous [...] because everything to her exists very much at the moment. I sometimes envy people who are made in such a way that they need not think, at least not at all deeply. It is an inconvenient habit and produces ill manners.

Yours
F. Békássy

---

[8] Rupert Brooke was in Germany. In his letter to Noel on 2 May 1912 from Berlin, he says that he is struggling with conflicting feelings between her and Ka Cox, *Song of Love*, pp.165-172.

[9] Békássy is referring to the manuscript mentioned already in his letter of 6 April 1912.

Letter 11 – 18 July 1912

Kis Sennye, Rum, Vas vm.

18 July 1912

Dear Noel,

Nothing much happened on the journey; we drove down to Oxted,[1] talking: the rain stopped and I did not get wet. It was shorter than I thought it would be. I arrived here in the evening [...].

And hurriedly put off my overcoat and shook off the dust on my feet against all England, Limpsfield only excepted. Cambridge got most of it. I am here with my sisters [...] now, the rest of the tribe are still in the land of shadowy existences. Meanwhile we see much of all sorts and conditions of men, and I am really beginning to like the way people go on here, i.e. in the Country: the town society is too atrocious.

Isn't it rather strange that all these people with immense capacities, and brains - well!!- should just gradually settle down on their land, manage it, think a good deal, read a good deal, the country *nemes*[2] gentlemen - and <u>never</u> produce anything! I shall be like that when I am 30; it's rather a pleasing prospect: a fruit farm or something, in a wild part of the country.

The people who do things here are not of the old families; superficially cultured, usually quite worthless. Well, let them! - as long as we others can keep our position, i.e. not have to work too much. - I was out on the river all yesterday, by myself, bathing, and in a boatlet (!) - it's really rather fun, one sees so many beasts: I got quite near to two grey herons and saw a fox catch a pheasant –but I think the bird must have been lame. It was frightfully sudden; the pheasant was strutting about on the

---

[1]   Oxted, Surrey, is the nearest railway station to Limpsfield (the Olivier residence).

[2]   '*nemes*', nobleman in Hungarian.

edge of the water and there were willows behind it.

I also found a log of 'rába-wood' (Rába is the river's name) i.e. wood that has been in the Rába long, gets black through and through, shiny, and very hard. Not far from here there is a place where the dining room is panelled and furnished with it, it really looks very fine. [...]

They are mending the mill and boxes and things have come to light: one immediately thinks of Pauly's ghost stories etc. One about the hairy hand might do. Or do you know the one in Shakespeare (!) 'It was not so'- 'and God forbid that it should be so'.[3] That's a very good one, too. As a matter of fact they were probably washed down by the water 30-40-50 years ago? That - mill is a dreadful concern! - But I must not begin lamenting about these things, there are so many to lament about: cherries, peaches, apples have all been frozen, every wretched tree is beginning to dry up; only the corn holds good - and the grapes, perhaps, in the other place. I very much want to be there for the vintage, but I don't know how to manage, Cambridge begins Oct. 10, which is a few days too early.

I have discovered a new poem - Hungarian - that I really and altogether like. There are some I always carry in my head (I don't mean know) but I chance on a new one that I could add to them so seldom, it is quite an event. There were those old French things: the '*À basse voix vous pris merci dame*' of Froissart[4] that I found by chance in a huge tome of rubbish and erudition in the Univ(ersity) Lib(rary).: '*Childe Roland to the Dark Tower came*',[5] we read at Justin's with Peter Watson last winter - and so forth. You've a share in one of them: 'Under a wide and starry sky'[6] which you wrote down for me once at Bedales in

---

[3]   Quotation from Act I Scene 1 of *Much Ado about Nothing*.

[4]   Jean Froissart (1337-1405?) French poet.

[5]   'Childe Roland to the Dark Tower came', poem by Robert Browning.

[6]   Poem 'Requiem' by Robert Louis Stevenson, Scottish poet (1850-1894), a favourite of Noel Olivier.

the Library! But there are lots by now - perhaps even thirty: only I don't know how I came by some of them. If they get many more I shall write them down in a book. Having them is a dangerous business, one's ideas change and then one keeps liking things like 'Pray but a prayer for me' (Morris)[7] because one did once. However.

How is Rupert behaving?[8] And: -?-?-?-?-?-? (These are the questions I would ask, if there was room).

Yours
F. Békássy
Békássy Feró
To be Hungarian

---

[7] Quotation from 'Summer Dawn' poem by William Morris (1834-1896) artist and poet.
[8] Brooke was staying in Grantchester. Noel had written to him on 13 July 1912 to tell him that Adrian Stephen, (brother of Virginia Woolf), had proposed to her, and that she had turned him down, *Song of Love* p. 192.

Rupert Brooke in 1913

Letter from Noel to Rupert Brooke –
2 August 1912

The following letter is from Noel to Rupert Brooke, at around this time, written from holiday in Switzerland. In it she tries to analyse her feelings towards Brooke, explaining why it is she cannot feel love towards him. Though we have no way of knowing what Noel was writing to Békássy, from his replies we can surmise that these words could easily apply to her attitude towards him.

We have deliberately left Noel's inaccurate spelling as it appears in the original.

Blumlisalp
Griesalp
Kientl
Berner Oberland

[2 August 1912]

Mon pauvre Vieux!

You'll be twenty five before this reaches you, and that will make you more you more forlorne than ever. When they read my character in childhood [...] they said: "Heart-hard. Hard as nails!" I grinned with pride, and never forgot, and people sans heart - or hard - they also say [...] can never really understand other people. But we can see something, a little, even with atrophied feelings and *peu de cervel.*[1] I see this much - But la! what help a list of what I see. It is so much of what you feel, that when I am absorbed in it, when I happen to drop into your position - as remembering your voice expressing it, or reading your letter, I become as hope-less as you, seeing no chance of any good, unless you marry me, see that it is grey

---

[1]   Peu de cervelle - little brains.

and a horrible waste, the ghastliest thing: a mistake, if that vague thing - the *chance* that we should once be together and confidant - should suddenly quite deffinitely be abolished. If all these times that we have known one another have helped build up such possibility and have depended on it, then they help now to make dreariness, becuase you were depending on them, and they turn out to be - what? (But here I cant see any more from you - my own very deffinite belief in the good of the times we've had sways you). But I think you are stranded somehow - quite what did it, I don't know; there has been a hope disappointed, and a certainty of clear good outraged. So you can say nothing but arguments and complaints, and do nothing but bemoan. And clearly you can take no joy in the other things which still go on. O, I hope they dont irritate you beyond endurance. I'm sure that you must keep up, plunge a bit and then get another footing. I know you will ultimately be strong to deal with all this nonsense: la Vie - pah!

I'm wretched and perplexed (tho' I still eat well - go about with cheerful mien) that it should be me who has failed you so horribly, I could curse and bully any other person and so get some satisfaction. But I see that I am right too; and that there should be any inevitable cause for this horror - oh so intensifies it. My dear I would be tortured in revenge for it, but I could not prevent it. It is so strong, the feeling that I mustn't marry you. It has grown up for years; side by side with the things that bind us (which you wrote of) other moments came, making me more and more sure that I did not love. I saw nothing to hate, which you could possibly change, it was the mean in me, which picked out bit by bit, parts of you - deffinitely and unalterably yours - to find fault with and ultimately to hate. If you knew the littleness of these components of dislike, you couldn't understand that they should count so, they are things which ought not be noticed - not allowed consideration - You would be right, because you are bigger than I am. But I cant put aside the nigglyness in myself, it has the greatest power over me, to ruin any good I could have to do with, and to cause the utterest misery, since I should know it was meanness winning: It could defile all the splendour you brought near me. That would be the worst. That shalnt ever be allowed to happen.

Rupert you mustnt die or go mad, or be dreary, just because Noel is romantic and petty - surely *now* you see how petty. You pass it, dispise it and go on. Its too miserable to be allowed to hurt you. I am so ashamed and so sorry that you thought I was at all tolerable. I know that my existence is shocking. I am too disgusting to go about at all, to be capable of hurting good people.

I muttered about it before. Tie pins and a profession are all I'm fit for. Tie pins for affection (Lord, it has led me astray!) and medicine for raison d'etre. With those I shall achieve all the happiness I am capable of. The better things need passion: and passion is not latent in me, it never grew there - at best I mourn it.

[continued next day]

Bless me! What stuff that is that I wrote yesterday. You may as well see it all, it probably signifies something.[…]

I cant be coherent.

You must wake up.

from Noel
August, 3rd

Letter 12 – 19 August 1912

Kis Sennye, Rum, Vas vm.
Hungary

19 August 1912

Dear Noel,

My congratulations to Bryn,[1] my most utter bewilderment, my astonishment, excitement, curiosity! (You did not say, to *whom!*) It was very good of you to put it all in the midst of descriptions of Salisbury Plain and Swiss hotels, - it was certainly the most effective way. I simply jumped! And am now busy imagining her all over again, because everything must be quite different; and am subject to her permission, tremendously pleased! (She won't mind if I've written this here instead of to her. Does she?)

I was already very pleased, having just returned from Bozsok[2]. You can't imagine what that means. I had been getting choked up with wanting to do things when there was nothing to do, wanting to write when I couldn't etc.: then I went for three days to a gentleman artist[3] I know and his wife and three small girls who among the mountains. She is not Hungarian, a German, but chiefly Italian and thinks, and he is an artist - but Hungarian, and both are utterly cultured and have better taste than anyone I know, so that everything in or about the house is better than one would think possible, and Tonika has been there for a fortnight because she wasn't well here and so I went to visit her. They made me stay and we talked and walked and flew kites with the two elder girls and it was all heather and young birch and rocks - and I hadn't talked for near seven weeks previously. Oh, we weren't above the ordinary standard, and I did not talk intellectual things much,

---

[1]   Alluding to Brynhild Olivier, Noel's sister's engagement to A.E. Hugh Popham.
[2]   Bozsok, village in Hungary near the Austrian border.
[3]   'a gentleman artist' refers to Békássy's cousin Gyula Végh, see Letter 1, footnote 5.

because two of them were artists there; and we even invented a new way of talking about other people, - or we only revived it - namely, one thinks of an animal, plant, smell, stone dish, musician, painter, colour fitting for a person. It is very good. Just think: 'a bird-of-paradise-and-red satin lady, Champagne (poured out) and a thoroughbred; or a smell of suede gloves, or of old galoshes, or of old ends of cigars! A brown bear, a grasshopper, a sparrow, - try making up something for the people you know! --

I *do* know *Wuthering Heights*[4] and like it (I had better begin writing about books so as not to get too wild) and I am glad you do so much that it is sure to have a place among your mental collection of books you don't forget about - but I hope Cambridge are not going to take it up, because they don't like *Prunella*[5] nor the *Forest Lovers*[6] nor Bédier's *Tristan et Isolde*[7] and are a set of baggages, and don't deserve to get such a book to play with. But then the other people, who like Bédier - etc. really don't care at all whether it's good or not, and think 'Porphyria' Browning's best poem, and I can't talk with them because they only understand the things one *doesn't* say. (They are artists whom you don't know)

In other words, Cambridge people ~~are~~ think, always, as a habit, and can think - poor things, how they get tied into knots, or how they torture themselves constantly, to evade being tied up and like that (that's what I do). But they consequently are gloomy and have bad characters. That's possibly so! but they can't bear any weight ~~and~~ nor do anything, while I am as strong as a bullock or a Bishop ('Rome, 15-')[8] with nerves to match. But then, the Cambridge people are perhaps more

---

4   Novel by Emily Brontë (1847).
5   Title of an Italian tale in *The Grey Fairy Book* (1900) by Andrew Lang.
6   Romantic historical novel (1898) by Maurice Henry Hewlett.
7   Novel by Joseph Bédier (1864-1934) French writer and critic.
8   Allusion to Browning's poem 'The Bishop orders his Tomb at St. Praxed Church (Rome,15-)'.

clearly thinkers, and someone must be that, I suppose. Then those other people are Perfecti, Cathari,[9] etc., and I adore them, because their 'I like' or 'I dislike' has more in them than anybody's reasoning, and their characters are always perfect, because they hardy know they've got one, so they're always pleasant to be with. But they can't think. How do you manage to do quite a decent amount of thinking without torturing yourself about it in the least! Voilá!

But of course, I am writing about books.

So Bryn and Margery[10] heard Childe Roland twice on two successive days, and I hope listened too much to the poem to compare the readers or I shall look foolish. Like David[11] dancing.

I don't give much for your forecast of my future. As for your pious aspirations about the Convent. I (almost) share them(!) I know a girl who was in a French one till this year, and she astonished me by saying she would very much like to go back: - because she is quite clever and lively (pigeon: a strongish blue; the smell of hay).

They all like it, I'm told; but it *does* mean being cut off from a lot of things we have and ~~consider~~ undervalue because they are often obnoxious.

Cambridge also appreciates the aristocratic eye. This, at least, was a Cambridger's reason for preferring other people to a certain philosopher.

'He's arrogant and full of cant;
They're elegant, they're elegant.'
- and he sees a man must *be* nice too.
'We do not like
A monkey on a motorbike.'

---

9   The Cathari were a Manicheistic sect which flourished in France in the 12th and 13th Centuries. 'Perfecti' were those Cathars, who reached the stage of 'perfection' through self-denial.
10 Noel's sisters.
11 Meaning King David of the Old Testament.

(I think the verses are Lord Shove's.[12] ~~Don't~~ he'll be angry if he knows I've told you. - A new light?)

And since I'm writing down verses - I find I'll do well for an Elizabethan or Jacobean poet, with such things as this, for a complaint of the deceived husband.

If seems no seeming, none but 'seems to see'.

Say seeming seems: seems seen some seem to be.

O pain plain paining! Pains poor pity's idea:

Pays pain complaining, pain plain 'noes' pay me?[13]

- or is that 'saying things too simply?

You see I am unemployed and looking for a post. I might write more. I feel myself able to do anything from standing on my head to writing a 'double ballad' about plants, in which the flowers would *all* have good manners, and the trees would all be slim and perfectly graceful. But as a matter of fact I do nothing. I haven't touched a book since 'Ekkehard'[14] except to admire the binding (Bozsok).

Today, it being the King's birthday, [Franz Joseph of Hungary] I went to hear the Bishop say mass. A lot of gentlemen were there in full *díszmagyar*,[15] fur, feathers, swords and all: and I could see

... The altar, on the epistle-side,

And up into the aery dome where live

The angels, and a sunbeam's sure to lurk

And somewhat of the choir ...[16]

and just hear the blessed mutter of the mass. *Per omnia saecula saeculorum!*[17] - I'm afraid we'll never be able to do that without our Church. People go there to admire a Bishop's stole

---

[12] Referring to Gerald Shove in jest as 'Lord'.

[13] Békássy's parody of Jacobean verse.

[14] *Ekkehard .Eine Geschichte aus dem 10. Jahrhundert* (1855) ('A Story from the 10th Century') is a historical novel by Joseph Victor von Scheffel.

[15] Ceremonial dress of the Hungarian nobility.

[16] A misquote of lines 21-24 of Browning's 'The Bishop orders his Tomb...'.

[17] Forever and ever (Latin).

perhaps, but that was always a good enough basis for the Pope's power - if there was enough money also. I stood next a very young gunner officer, who looked just like the hero in some very romantic novel; such perfect features, and fiery eyes, and glossy black hair, and that haughty yet light carriage - it's the first time I've seen somebody with *all* the essentials. I wonder if that sort of thing will happen to him?

[...]

All this time I am trying to think of what I would choose for you, and as, luckily, it happens to be quite flattering, I'll write it.

	What I think	What I might imagine *(But it isn't time. Would you like it?)*
Animal	Young trout	Young trout
Plant	Sweet Pea	Poppies
Colour	Mauve	A strong blue
Smell	Of salt air	Of fir cones
Stone *(need not be a precious stone)*	Opal	Pearl
Food	Sugar & Water	Sugar & Water

If you are very angry, tell me in the same way that you think of me. I'll see how it tallies with the Hungarian idea. Don't be led astray by popular qualities associated with things.

Yours
F. Békássy
(I would have blushed if you had written Feri.
Everyone writes it, so please don't!)

Letter 13 – 18 September 1912

Kis Sennye, Rum, Vas vm.

18 September 1912

Dear Noel,

Will you be in London or at Limpsfield or un-get-at-able when I return to Cambridge, that is to say on about Oct.10th? Because one can't get away very often after term begins and I would like to see you before I see Cambridge people, who are very nice etc, but *do* get on one's nerves. (All except Maynard,[1] who is staying here now and does not seem to be liking it very much, I'm afraid).

I shall see Peter Watson meanwhile! (This may be a secret, I don't know). The only other person I care [about] is Rupert. Do you know if he'll be in Cambridge next term?

History is extraordinary nonsense. Writing poetry is an extraordinary encumbrance, and annoying as it isn't good in the end. So what *is* one to do?

Yours
F. Békássy
Excuse laconical profusion. Please imagine
some decent scenery as I haven't described any.

---

[1]   Maynard Keynes is visiting the Békássy family home in Hungary.

Letter 14 – 21 October 1912

King's.

21 October [1912] Monday

Dear Noel,

Forgive the sugar and water! You will do it more easily if you think of all the other things, and Rupert's poem about the trout![1]

I <u>never</u> said your predictions were cranky! I only said they were wrong: like Isaiah, not like Habakkuk! These new ones I suppose were right; though the Russians are moving across the Caucasus and if there is war and if we Hungarians are in danger of becoming a province of Austria again, or if the King dies,[2] or if Saturn is in conjunction with Mars, I shall go and fight.

But this, of course, is just the 'Balkan trouble'[3] to English people: I can imagine T.J.G.[4] very proud of himself - his prophecies, and giving one lecture a week about it all.

Splendid the Montegrines were! Do you know that last year the forts round the lake of Scutari had been declared far too strong for them and Russia had on that ground forbidden an expedition of theirs into Scutari?[5] They looked in pretty bad places too, as far as one was allowed to see. I have been with Peter [Grant Watson] in Paris; he <u>is</u> such a rocket of a person! He pretends to be a fixed star now; but one can see from the way he scintillates that he isn't really. He is going to write - stories about the Bush: he showed me some and they were good! Besides, he's so good at imposing on people, he must succeed

---

[1]   Probably a reference to Brooke's poem 'The Fish'.
[2]   Emperor Franz Joseph of Austria, also King of Hungary.
[3]   The Balkan War had been declared by Montenegro against the Ottoman Empire on October 8, 1912, a few weeks before Békássy wrote this letter.
[4]   T.J.Garstang, history teacher at Bedales.
[5]   Town in Montenegro.

- if only he were in Town, instead of in Florence. He showed me, once more another best poem in the world:

> Had we but world enough and time   Marvell. See
> Your coyness, Lady, were no crime.[6]   (Oxford Book)

And going on in the most amazing way. They <u>are</u> usually the best poems in the world. So you see! I am very full of ideas, and so elated that it almost seems absurd. Then there is R. Catholicism, - you know everybody is being converted, Jaques is becoming Xtian. Gwen is one - against which I am all up in arms and keen to see it damned. J. and G., [Jaques and Gwen] by the way, are getting a house beyond Royston,[7] it'll be great fun.

So you see I am not in a state of quiescence , like I was last vac.; an immense number of things are happening every day, even if it is 'only' my seeing some tropical orchid (aristolochia). Do you <u>know</u> orchids? This one isn't like any other. [...]They are quite unhuman, unearthly, un-everything. I was in ecstasies and shall write a poem.

There is a darker side to everything of course; I have heard via Raisley about Dorothy and was very upset - you can imagine how it feels to one of my ideals to imagine her gradual domestication. Then there is Gotch who seems quite going to pieces in consequence of things that happened to him - he doesn't take them like Cambridge people (I ~~probably~~ include myself) who mope and get a nervous breakdown; but drinks and is wild. I don't know what to do. I wish I could do something - at any rate had been more intimate with him. Don't spread this; rumour's bad enough already and only makes things harder. I want to talk to Lapthorn who knows everything concerning it, ~~but~~ I don't care if it looks like meddling.

[...] I often think of Bedales now; Peter reminded me of it and our reading society which you must vividly remember; e.g.

---

6   Quotation from Andrew Marvell's poem 'To His Coy Mistress'.
7   Town near Cambridge.

The Master Builder or *The Lady from the Sea*[8] at Lumpet; and Bill[9] made me uncomfortably astonished by mentioning a scene in which I talked about 'expansion' etc., to him and you and Mary Newbury[10] during prep.

It is so absurd that I am very ashamed of it and very amused; and to think it probably happened during my last 3 years there!

Do you ever get letters from Mary? Or write to her?

Meanwhile I am writing or have written - but rather the latter than the former. I have written a huge essay on Browning and wanted to get the Members' Prize[11], (but is it bad?) because I think its methods are immensely sensible.

Rupert is reading my poems,[12] all of which are bad. It is terrible to write bad poetry. If I could write <u>one</u> quite good poem I would be quite a different person; so much less fitful and feeling just as much as now - and noticing much more at least of mere material things.

But it is easy to bear even though I like Maynard less than I did and Rupert is grand (at a safe distance). I don't mean he is less grand otherwise, but dangerous. I've got lots of things worth doing. I like to know queer Cambridge people just to get away from ~~our own~~ the usual rigid quite intellectual and precise behaviour. I like to know people outside Cambridge.

At present I feel as though, happen what may I shall never be moping and sighing again, and shall learn to be despairing, when I am despairing, in a decent way.

I am working. I shall read a paper soon on some medieval

---

8   'The Master Builder' and 'The Lady from the Sea', plays by Norwegian
    playwright Henrik Ibsen (1828-1906). It is unclear what or where 'Lumpet' is.
9   Probably William P. Burdet, fellow-pupil at Bedales.
10 Mary Newbery Sturrock (1892-1985) Scottish painter, at Bedales with Békássy
    and Noel.
11 In 1912, the Cambridge University Member's Prize, was in fact awarded to
    another student.
12 Rupert Brooke did read Békássy's poems, but returned them without comment.
    See Introduction and *Song of Love*, p. 229.

subject. I don't know what. Something about ideas: [...].

I <u>am</u> glad you have read some Arabian Nights![13] Aren't they immensely good! It is such a treat to have imagination, with which writers are usually the very reverse of lavish, heaped up on imagination until one simply can't go on. What the Sultan must have been like ~~by the sound of it~~! To stand 1001 nights! Go on reading them.

I would like to buy my tennis racquet myself. If you are going to be at Limpsfield next weekend I suppose you would be going down on Saturday by that midday train. Do write and answer.

Yours
Feri Békássy

---

[13]   *The Arabian Nights Entertainment*, first published in English in 1706, is better known by its later title *The One Thousand and One Nights*.

Letter 15 – 30 October 1912 (Summary)

In this letter from Cambridge, Békássy writes that he is still working on his Browning Essay. He complains that their last meeting [probably at Noel's home in Limpsfield] was 'all too short.' He says James Strachey had told him that he had fallen in love with a girl and Békássy guesses that the girl must be Noel. In a letter the following month, November, Noel tells Brooke that 'I almost committed suicide, when it turned out that 'Békássy had got it too (Love, love).'[1] Brooke scathingly replies a few weeks later that what Békássy has is 'calf-love' similar to that which he had felt for her.[2]

Letter 16 – 5 November 1912

King's

5 November 1912

Dear Noel,

I have just done with all the work I've been doing; I read my 'Pantheism'[3] paper yesterday - it seemed to go down very well - having written all of it the same day, though it is some 30 of my close pages. I had a very exciting and pleasant surprise at the end of it. Last year in connection with another paper,[4] I came across a man Sebastian Franck,[5] a 16th century humanist who hated the Reformation ('a contemptible monkish dispute)[6] and said Luther[7] had set up a Pope, after doing away with the

---

[1]   *Song of Love*, p. 228.

[2]   *Ibid*, p. 230.

[3]   'Pantheism', the belief that the Universe (nature) is identical with divinity.

[4]   We know from an earlier letter of Békássy's that the essay was entitled 'Reformation and Renaissance'.

[5]   Sebastian Franck (1499-1542/43) German historian, best known for *Chronica*,1531.

[6]   A quote from Thomas M. Lindsay, *A History of the Reformation*, Edinburgh, 1906, p. 77.

[7]   Martin Luther (1483-1546) German theologian, Father of the Protestant Reformation.

other one, and was a forerunner of people like Fr. Bacon,[8] and the most lovable man I know. - *Now*, I tried to show Pantheism meant absolutely anything and everything at different times. (the only connection between Pantheists being that they have the same cast of mind, and that they say the same, though they mean *utterly* different things)

I had got to the 16th century 'Libertines' and was disgusted. It was the end of the Middle Ages lingering on; these men believed in an eventual annihilation, said action was futile, said Human character, the sensual world, and thought was illusion; made Death their God (literally: they call Christ 'Death') and entirely lost hold of earth. I was upset: does Pantheism, which after all, sometimes gave rise to fine men of really living ideas, fizzle out like this?

Imagine my joy when I found Franck was a Pantheist. A new sort of Pantheist, going back to the Greeks, and modern at the same time! I went on reading him all Sunday; and consequently became very enthusiastic once more about my subject. Do you know he said history was accumulated human experience, to be used practically; and was the first to write it in the vernacular? Erasmus[9] simply isn't in it beside him!

Also at the beginning of last week I got my Browning essay[10] back from the College (with a prize - £5 in books! Just think what I am going to get!) and re-wrote it for the Members' Prize, (it is now being typed) - so you see as far as other people went - except Gotch - I was buried quite. He, of course, is doing splendidly. He has now entirely given up

---

[8]   Francis Bacon, Lord Verulam (1561-1626) English writer, philosopher, author of *Novum Organum*, 1620.
[9]   Erasmus of Rotterdam, influential philosopher, Dutch humanist and scholar (1466-1536). Spent time at Queen's College, Cambridge, where he introduced the study of Greek.
[10] The English version of this essay has been lost. A Hungarian version was found and published in Sennyey Weiner pp. 311-355.

drink and is working, and altogether getting over it. I saw Phyllis the other day - she seems to be enjoying Newnham a lot - and we talked about it. I wish I could see more of them; I haven't seen Alix[11] for *ages*.

A whole crowd of Bedalians are coming up for the *Play* on the 30th so you could see them; but perhaps you could come up on the day before, and stay longer, and so see something of people like Maynard - Rupert I am afraid will be in Germany. I wonder whether on the 30th I shall be able to get for lunch the people *I* want: for tea I am having a squash of 15 and there are bound to be some nice people among them.

Everything here has suddenly changed; a few sharp frosts, and instead of the blaze of colour by the Backs,[12] you have the yellow leaves or none or few and a general scarcity everywhere. Only the upper river is much the same, beyond Byron's pool:[13] I went for a long walk there once with one Alexander, a Quaker ornithologist,[14] in the evening - work seeming insupportable - we continually saw herons flapping along in the just gathering mist; and moorhens, out for seed on the fields, splash into the water as we went by. And queer little birds making an unholy noise in the hedges.

By the way, I saw Ka at the Cornfords, looking very splendid, and we - at least I - had rather a fine evening. You know it is a pity that I never see most of the people I am really pleased to be with, I shall go and see Jaques for some time when I haven't got to work. (And all this work *so* useless for the Tripos! As though I were not doing a stroke of work all day). Of course there is Bliss but he is now so exasperating and exasperated.

---

[11] Alix Sargant-Florence see Letter 3, footnote 10.

[12] Stretch of land behind the colleges along the riverside in Cambridge.

[13] Weir pool in Grantchester village near Cambridge, named after Lord Byron (1788-1824) who reputedly swam there while a student at Trinity College.

[14] Horace Gundry Alexander (1889-1989) ornithologist. At King's College until 1912.

Ka was so enthusiastic about the riding at Everleigh[15] that I must go down and see sometime next vac. It sounded very thrilling.

I must find a motto for my essay - I wish I could do that sort of thing? I would like it to be good.

I *have* had a few dreams but I can't remember who they are about. If you had any that are possible to tell, do write them to me. Also about your doings.

Maynard was in London a few days ago and came back very pleased with himself. On the whole I have the sort of feeling that nothing at all is happening anywhere.

'Now all is still, earth is a wintry clod'

[…]

'Till 'spring-wind like a dancing psaltress passes
over its breast to waken it'.[16]

Yours
F. Békássy

---

15 Village in Wiltshire, where, in the summer of 1912 one of the reading parties of
    John Maynard Keynes took place.
16 Two quotes from Robert Browning's poem 'Paracelsus'.

Letter 17 – 11 January 1913

The Chestnuts
East Isley, Berkshire

11 January 1913

(Cambridge begins on 14th)

Dear Noel,

I woke up this morning and wondered at the way I have been going on; or, (as my pride would make me put it) the way things have been happening: and I disapproved. It is at any rate unfortunate that, when I ought evidently to have seen something of you this Christmas, or should at least have had one or two letters, I should have made it at all impossible almost at the last moment.

Now, there is no prospect of my seeing you, for a long time. I do not mind - after all, I hardly ever see any of the people I care about - but I hope you will write to me, and that I will write to you also. For the latter will give me almost as much pleasure as the former. And especially in my present circumstances. I will try to say what these are, for although it is possible that you do not care, I think you do.

I don't know what you think about me. If you write, I will see - But perhaps it has been just as absurd to write this, as to write those other letters which when I now think of them make me 'blush inside' (and *hate* the thought that it is possible that someone may see them). - Perhaps it would have been better for me to write about my trip to Switzerland,[1] or say

---

[1]   In the letter to James Strachey dated 20 December [1912] included in this volume, Békássy writes of his planned visit to Switzerland to meet Peter Grant-Watson.

what Paris is like?[2] But I don't think I could have done. It all happened so strangely last term and so unfortunately. Or am I exaggerating, and do you think nothing happened at all? But I didn't think so, at the time. So, I can't just write as if it hadn't been. However, it is all horrid to think about.

I shall not now write about anything I've been doing lately, though there is plenty to say, but will leave that till afterwards.

Till then

Yours
F. Békássy

2   On the way back from Switzerland, Grant-Watson and Békássy spent two days in Paris, where they visited Gertrude Stein, who in a letter to a friend Mabel Lodge describes Békássy as 'a perfectly delightful Hungarian patriot poet… who is being educated in England.' Cf. Suzanne Falkiner, *The Imago, E.L.Grant-Watson and Australia*, UWA Publishing, Crawley, Western Australia, 2011, p. 196.

Letter 18 – February 1913

King's College, Cambridge

[end February 1913]

Dear Noel,

Thank you very much for the way you made everything go so smoothly last Thursday, and especially that you did not show whatever sympathy you felt and so made me much more quiet and containing myself. You see (I hope) that I can behave in quite a decently ordinary way though when I think of it the subjects of our conversation were very curious perhaps.

I stayed after you went away until my train went - [...]

There are many things I ought to be doing now and the sight of Maynard should certainly inspire me with a desire to work. *He* says he is working 8 or 9 hours a day and as *I* know he sleeps 11 not much is left, so that he is getting quite used to never seeing anybody and if he were to go on like this would, he says, hate human society in a few months' time. Besides, I am having a revulsion from using my brain for thinking - which should also help my Tripos work! Altogether I can't understand - do you, for instance, really like doing brain work? Aren't most women - of course I am only talking of all intelligent ones - better fit to do other things with their brain, for instance Ka [Cox]. However that may be *we* have no choice, you in your Science and Work and I in my Philosophy and its Critical surroundings. However in two weeks' time I shall be at home I hope but perhaps only in the town. I think I shall work but anyhow it will be good - and the riding! And seeing quite many people whom I want to see. But I wish that Jaques was back here, neither he nor the Cornfords are: they disappeared suddenly, some time ago.

It is curious living in a College with all sorts of corporate movements and with as very different sets as King's: the intricacy of intrigues would please anyone - though now we have seem to have got to a state of things where everyone leaves everyone else alone and no one is very keen on the ordinary Societies - all of which seems to me very civilised, people do learn to leave each other more alone than they used to.

[…]

I meant to go down to Bedales but I don't think I shall because I am not quite well and don't much want to see anyone (except my Tribe,[1] and will see them all in a little time: including the Zurich one and the 5 people of as many Nationalities with whom he lives!)[2] […].

Yours
F. Békássy

---

[1] 'Tribe' his siblings still at Bedales.
[2] His brother István Békássy was studying in Zürich.

Letter 19 – 6 March 1913

[Cambridge]

Thursday, 6 March 1913

Dear Noel,

To sound off the term in as pleasant a way as possible, I went to Croydon on Thursday, and saw Gwen and Jacques. I wonder if you have seen their house yet: it is a splendid place all in the middle of fields, on a hill, with a vast view down Southwards, and the most violently boisterous wind blowing all the time I was there. It is hard to imagine how pleasant it must be for them, and they working hard and full of things to create. Gwen is painting pictures of which I hardly know how to speak. Especially one of Mary and Elizabeth,[1] and a Christ in the Garden, and a portrait of Jacques' father; I have never seen any picture of whose greatness I felt so sure! And of course I was altogether moved by them. She already has the assurance which only really great artists have, who know that nothing else matters. - This makes me think of Keats' letters: the ones he wrote in his last two years; full of what one cannot call insolence, but pride coming from certainty, because he knows he is expressing ideas that make up the world, and that his poems are not merely expressions of his feelings, but are individual things. - This is a question of which I talked with Jacques, and was very glad to find he agreed with the conclusion I have only lately made, namely that theories of art have been absurd chiefly because they have not taken the picture into account; which may in a secondary way express the artist's feelings, or may have his character, but is primarily a Thing not connected with the artist or the onlooker - you may call it the expression of a metaphysical idea (I think a metaphysical

---

[1]   The Virgin Mary and Elizabeth, Mother of St. John the Baptist.

reality is the same) if you like. - Jacques of course is rather restless because he can only work three hours or so a day; but he too is settling down, I mean becoming more certain of the ways in which he can work. Of course he is not like Gwen, but still good: and they both use such colours! I saw some dancing figures he had painted, and they are better beyond comparison than Duncan's[2] which you saw in Maynard Keynes' room.

As you may guess, I have been reading poetry. When you said bad poetry was so very bad and there was so much of it, I wonder did you include 'the bad poetry of great poets?' I find myself getting more and more lenient towards it, in this sense only, that I am reconciled to its existence because it has so many interests. In this March number of the *English Review,* have you read 'Aphrodite at Leatherhead' by a new poet called Helston?[3] I hardly like to speak of it, because it somehow seems not to stand broad daylight, and I almost wonder how he published it. In a way I think it very very good but it is not at all, really; and whenever I think of it without looking at it, it seems hopelessly bad in sentiment. But - well, what would you have said of 'Endymion'[4] when it came out? Bad, no doubt, with dreadful faults of taste and dreadful sentiment. I think I would have treasured it up a good deal, and not talked about it, and looked forward to any other poem. This young man Mr. Keats might write, which would not be 'a feverish attempt rather than a deed accomplished'[5] (But that is only supposing I had not read the 1817 poems, which - most of them - are really too absurd for words. -) I dare say you will just be disgusted at John Helston's 'feverish attempt', but - well it is not profitable to prophesy.

---

[2] Duncan Grant (1885-1978) painter, John Maynard Keynes's friend and long-time lover. Together with painter Vanessa Bell (1879-1961), later his partner, he painted a mural in King's College, Cambridge.

[3] John Helston (1877-1928?) English poet, writing before and during World War I.

[4] 'Endymion' (1818) poem by John Keats.

[5] Quote from Preface to above.

Most of the poetry I've been reading is Hungarian, modern, and good - a great literary movement began some six years ago, which is creating quite a new poetry - and also classics and still better, namely John Arany,[6] the one Hungarian poet whom I think as great as Goethe or Dante. His greatest poems are what he calls Ballads, and they are - well, can you imagine a lyrical poem which has the same effect as Shakespeare's Tragedies have?

I shall be at home very soon, thank God, and then when I am not continually hearing <u>and talking</u> a foreign language, I may be better able to write in my own. I am also intending to work, but …! A week before Easter Sunday we move out of the town, and the rest is perpetual joy. But especially, if before I come back we are to get the usual hot week or two, and I can bathe the whole length of the river.

Next term General Shove[7] won't be up here, and I suppose Rupert won't come; so really (except for ordinary and accidental purposes) Bliss and myself will be a good deal more dependent on each other than hitherto. You know, he is changing such a lot, and getting over his culturedness, so that one sees more and more plainly what a good character he has. Also I like him a great deal and can get on well with him—at least relatively to the way I get on with most Cambridge people.

I am now also finding it is very queer to imagine what things will be like when one's sister gets married, as Tonika will do, though I am not sure how soon. In a way I am very glad, I like him very much, - though I don't know him well; and Tonika was so miserable about it before—but being at home without her will be strange.

---

[6] János Arany (1817-1882) Hungarian poet, author of the epic poem 'Toldi' and of historical ballads. Johann Wolfgang Goethe (1749-1832) author of 'Faust', Dante Alighieri (1265-1321) Italian poet, author of 'The Divine Comedy'.

[7] 'General', probably a pun on Shove's first name Gerald. See Main Characters.

I forgot to say what a walk back I had from Croydon, - it is some 12 miles or so, as I came, straight across fields all the way. It was 6 o'clock before I started and dark soon: I did not know there was such uninhabited country round Cambridge. Miles and miles of footpath or track without a light visible: I met no one except in the villages I passed, and from Hazlingfield to Grantchester might have been in a desert but for one farm, which showed no signs of being inhabited. - I had never been that way and was very proud of finding my way (having merely looked at a map before I started) -

Another thing I am proud of is that yesterday I heard a paper by Mr. A.C Benson[8] on Realism in Fiction, in which he disparaged Romantics and praised Realists; and he had to admit, in discussion that followed, that by Realists he had meant Romantics who did not commit some faults common to all bad novelists! So I have had my share in destroying the Enemies of God!

Yours
F. Békássy

---

[8]   Arthur C. Benson (1862-1925) taught English Literature, Fellow, later Master of Magdalene College, Cambridge.

Letter 20 – 21 March 1913

Kis Sennye, Rum, Vas vm.

Friday, 21 March 1913

Dear Noel,

I had to stand the 'way you behaved', hadn't I? You couldn't do anything else. It is all very simple and plain, and - well, is there anything one can say about it? I was as well at Bryn's afterwards, as anywhere else. (*Mais j'y pense trop, à cet après-midi.*)[1] I do envy you in this that - if I am right - you are always more or less calm without extremes of feeling. I hate myself for being so changeable and full of moods, that to settle down to anything is impossible. I want calm, because otherwise we - <u>can't</u> write poetry. As you say, I did a poem, last Monday and so was calm and even for 2 whole days, before, so that I should be able to write, and one after, because everything except the poem seems insignificant. Even if it doesn't turn out to be what one wishes, there is a peculiar joy in seeing one's <u>own</u> feelings frozen into a stanza which has nothing to do with one, when it has once been written. Imagine Wordsworth, writing of Lucy's death: -

'No motion has she now, no force;

She neither hears nor sees -

Whirled round in earth's diurnal course,

With rocks, and stones, and trees'.[2]

You see the distinction between what his feeling about her death probably was, and the meaning of this as a poem?

I wrote my poem because I was alone in Sennye (very alone, and it isn't a village, and no one is working on the fields) which

---

[1] But I think back too much to that afternoon (French).
[2] Békássy misquotes the poem 'Lucy' by William Wordsworth(1770-1850); third line should read 'Roll'd round…' not 'Whirled round'.

you have described so well that I need not: only that the horses are lame; and that a cyclone passed right over us - it must have come via the south of England - so that in 3 hours <u>everything</u> changed from warm spring to winter: there was a snowstorm, and for more than a day everything was white - 3 inches of snow! then a very little secondary rain, and now it is splendid and sunny. But now my family have come, or some of them, and I want to be alone and am all ups and downs again. I am living in poetry now, and wish I had not to go back to Cambridge. I <u>don't</u> fit in, although I like everybody. But how grand for you to go climbing among the Lakes!

'These tourists, heaven preserve us! needs must live
A profitable life!'[3]

(The poem proceeds by comparing them to butterflies!)

Meanwhile Tonika's betrothal (we are in Hungary) is to be on Easter Sunday. Not many of either our, or His relations, will be there, but still, it is something of a festive occasion. I don't as yet know any of his family. Him I like very much, he is very generous, full of splendid 'temperament', and always a little at war with the world. - Of course I shall see less of Tonika - but that is only after the summer. She won't be <u>very</u> far away at first; but as he is in the army, one never knows. This also makes the (I still think, inevitable, - and perhaps very useful) war with Russia a question of some anxiety. ....

My ambition is becoming <u>immense</u>, I hardly dare to think of it. I am continually discontented because I want to accomplish. I always find I am not much good at this or that. <u>What </u>is going to become of me, and <u>what</u> am I to do?! It is this absolute indecision which takes hold of me so; and makes me waste my time.

Tell me why feelings I write down sound absurd? Can real

---

[3] First two lines of Wordsworth's 'The Brothers'.

feelings not be said in words and are beasts better off because they can grunt and squeal them? And musicians, because they do the same (I am told)? Or is there anything repulsive in vaguely saying them? I have always assumed I wanted everyone to know everything (except one, of which I am <u>too</u> ashamed) about me - and that I ought to know everything about everyone else! It seems perfectly clear that this ought to be the only way of getting on with people at all! Of course any feeling I have is only mine and though people should all know it in order to fit themselves to it (I would do the same) yet it is not itself any concern of theirs (except when it is about them). I am, however, strong enough - supposing they do not observe this, to enforce it, and I hate all this 'sensitive' weakness. Then - why am I beginning to care a little for privacy and secrecy? Of course there are obvious cases e.g. when people's feelings would be, and I <u>definitely want them not to be</u>, hurt: but these are rare.

All this has no concern with anything in the world, except me in a general sort of way! ...

So you saw the *Spectre de la Rose*[4] again? I hope you were i.e. thunderstruck, both times. And about the Pictures; I saw the narrow "Gethsemane" finished, and the broad one being made - has the earlier, after all, turned out to be the better of the two? And have you seen the Mary and Elizabeth one?[5] - As for interrupting, 12 miles and mud are really mostly what prevents me from doing it oftener!

[...]

It is now getting dark - which, (from my high window to the west and the meadows) is romantic enough, but - when the

---

[4] 'Le Spectre de la Rose' ballet created for Vaslav Nijinsky, choreography Michel Fokine for Diaghilev's Ballets Russes and premiered in Monte Carlo in April 1911. Based on a poem by French poet, Theophile Gautier (1811-1872).

[5] Paintings by Jaques Raverat, 'Gethsemane' garden where Jesus went to pray the night before his crucifixion. 'Mary and Elizabeth', see previous letter.

lamp is not yet cleaned and brought up - prevents one going on. Otherwise I might continue indefinitely

Yours
F. Békássy

By the way, do you know '*Cyrano de Bergerac*' (by Rostand)[6] I was looking at it again. It is really great fun. And you don't read German, do you?

Give Jacques my love and say I want to see him, before I sink into my four-weeks Oblivion. He wasn't in.

---

[6] Play by Edmond Rostand (1868-1918) performed with great success in Budapest in Hungarian.

Letter 21 – 31 March 1913

Kis Sennye, Rum, Vas vm.

31 March 1913

Dear Noel,

I was very sad you haven't got to the Lakes, till I found (at the end of your letter) that you hoped to go there anyhow, as soon as your temperatures allowed, which I hope is now. And anyhow you don't seem to have got tired of Limpsfield lanes re to judge by your descriptions! - I always remember it as raining: - this isn't ungrateful of me, because I like it most of all in the rain and haze, which fits it better than it does this countryside: a plain always looks best in bright weather. But that reminds me, I am writing this almost as one writes a Testament, tomorrow I am going away with my brother to uninhabited parts. A cart with empty sacks and things and ourselves, will start tomorrow at 4 in the morning: and soon we will be on the hills that lie east of us - all heather and birch trees, and then we will 'trek' all day, through forest and meadow, passing a 'wilderness' in which there is nothing but bare hills, not even proper grass, and a few white flints and one or two wretched prickly plants: and finally just before sunset, one gets to the top of a hill and sees the Garden of Paradise, a long, low ridge covered with beech, a well and a spring; a lot of greenery and peach trees and pears - a farm house, a thatched hut, and perhaps two teams of buffaloes.- It is a place some of which belongs to us, and to others but no one lives there, beyond the people who work it. The thousands of acres all round, which are desert, belong I am glad to say, to the Church.

I have been there once, but only for a very little while, and it is still full of mysteries. Just now, too, there will be so many flowers - in short, just about the time, as Goethe says, 'Spring

begins in earnest';[1] (if you won't take his word for it - all his
critics, you know, agree that it is one of the most certainly true
things he has said - only the questionable authority of a doubtful
Canonical forgery, the Calendar, remains.) - and what doesn't
begin with it? - There is no question about my liking a 'placid'
letter - but I really <u>don't</u> need soothing! Of course, I can't get
out of it, I did say that I envy your calmness: I meant it too,
because sudden vacillations and 'splendid feelings' are not real
energy: but why not be all the same full of eagerness? You see,
everything has conspired to make me arrogant, and the result
has been that in everything which interests me, I now know
what it is that I want! And so it really matters less than before,
what I get. - I am not going to write about my Cambridge
work, because I would have to admit that I am no good and a
hopeless slacker, which would lower me in my self-esteem(!) - I
do find all the general part silly! The way it would be really
splendid to do it, is like Bellot ma[jor][2] who is now in Rome
(where every Tourist goes to see Classical Antiquity) doing the
history of Renaissance Italy, and lunching with Nobles whose
names he knows from his Books! - Miss Lamb[3] told me this
when I was at Bedales, I went there at the end of last term and
found to my great joy that people are waking up a little, and
especially that the Sergeant[4] has been sacked! Perhaps as a
reaction from last term, I have spent all my time in some sort
of exercise, tennis or fooling about in boats, or trying to shoot
wild duck (an innocent pastime!) and of course riding, alone,
or with Tonika when He[5] isn't here, which is not often now. -

---

[1] Johann Wolfgang Goethe (1749-1832) probably referring to a line in 'Frühling
     übers Jahr'.
[2] Hugh Hale Bellot (1890-1969) pupil of Bedales, historian, later Professor of
     University College, London. Here 'ma' i.e. 'major' refers to the fact that he was
     the elder of two brothers at the school.
[3] Miss H. E. Lamb teacher at Bedales.
[4] 'The Sergeant' nickname of an unidentified teacher at Bedales.
[5] 'He' Antonia's husband.

I wonder (apropos of your inky-faced dog) whether little boys here are as funny as at Limpsfield. when they see Tonika riding, (side-saddle) they shout: look, the lady hasn't got any legs!

[…]

What Literature you have been reading - I wonder what you made of Shakespeare's poetry. You know the Sonnet beginning 'Let me not to the marriage of true minds'? cxvi,[6] (I think) - if you want to read classics, I think 'Paradise Regained' wouldn't be a bad idea, it is much too often maligned - or if you don't read it all, there is a short passage, the description of a feast, towards the end of Bk II: 'A Table richly spread, in regal mode' - with something about the Knights of <u>Logres</u> or of <u>Lyones</u>, or <u>Pelleas</u>, or <u>Pellenore</u> - it is as good as any thing in 'Paradise Lost'.[7] I am at last, with saner mind, beginning to understand Wordsworth (things like 'The Leech Gatherer', 'The Brothers' or 'Michael')[8] - and this I regard as a sign that as far as English Literature is concerned, my being foreign does not mean that I understand it less than English people!

Tonika has been getting a lot of letters of congratulation with some very queer ones - we always laugh at them though it is wicked, because one will probably have to write them oneself sometime, or condoling! still worse.

- I must go and arrange about what we are to take with us, how I will wake up tomorrow, I don't know. We intend to walk back, a different way - if there is enough time. On the 11th of April I shall again be at Cambridge, under the humiliating necessity of swotting for an exam.

Yours

F. Békássy

---

6   William Shakespeare's Sonnet 116.
7   'A Table richly spread, in regal mode…' line 340 from Book II of Milton's *Paradise Regained* (1671).'Knights of Logres' (etc) are lines 360 and 361 of the same work.
8   Poems by William Wordsworth.

Letter 22 – 18 April 1913

Cambridge

[18th April 1913]

Dear Noel,

You will not mind my writing, though I have not yet had a letter from you. I wonder if you did get to the Lakes in the end. But if not, at least you have seen Peter Watson: I wonder what you think of him! He is still making exciting things happen to him, and as for ideas! - but no doubt he will have told you enough about himself. Last winter I saw two stories he had written, both <u>very good</u> indeed! But there were many bad ones too.

Did you like him when we read plays at Bedales and I was mad about him? I went to see Murray[1] yesterday (I wonder how much of him you remember - from those impossible preps about Cicero!) and was - as always - very impressed. Just think, someone who keeps his eyes open, knows his own mind about everything, cares about nothing which does not concern him! And so very evidently fit for a place in the order of things! - Whereas I - it is partly the fault of my family (my mother's family)

In each generation there are one or two persons in it who are carrying on the same thread. Each is like his father, and his father's father etc. The Family is almost consciously trying to evolve a Man. It can't do it. - I have been reading a notebook of my grandfather's.[2] He, like all the others, was a man of <u>very</u> great intelligence; <u>wise</u>, not talented or accomplished, but with a vein of three or four talents. Of very great sympathy; very forcible feelings: [...] He should have <u>made</u> a place for himself in the order of things. But 'is it possible that a man who cannot take sides in the greatest issues known to me, can

---

[1]   G. Murray fellow pupil at Bedales.
[2]   Maternal grandfather, Elek Bezerédj (1823-1894).

do work of lasting value? - It is not possible'. (This is Mazzini[3] and I believe it) - He tried many things, finished none: then retired on his land and brooded further on the nature of things. [...] I have read an unfinished notebook of his; he wrote part of an essay, a few sad and unsuccessful fragments of poetry. I believe he destroyed a lot of other things. - His daughter in the course - and so on, like a genealogical list in Genesis. One could write a novel about one of them. There are plenty to choose: six generations for certain: I think the thread goes through all the twenty-four. -

I am sorry I have written so much about my grandfather: it took rather a long time to say.

Here I was interrupted by a pleasant young man of this college, who came in very dejected. I gave him tea and made him argue about politics (his favourite subject). Eventually he went away. -

Coming over to England I stayed in a little German town with old squiggly-tiled roofs and a lot of painted wood on the houses; also a <u>semi-romane</u>sque (double) church tower which is <u>perfect</u> (a thing that doesn't often happen in architecture.) Even the tram-conductors looked medieval (to my enraptured eyes). I went for a long walk in the country round it - a landscape of greys and browns, with birches here and there like vellum-bound books on a shelf. (One could imagine quite a good landscape out of a bookshelf.) I saw a sudden and complete snow storm, it behaved itself in the most approved meteorological fashion! Till I got here I felt <u>so</u> continental! But it wore off very soon: though I have not seen many people yet - except Bliss, who is ill, and half the college is to be found in his room entertaining him. I made him very angry today by saying (talking of poetry) that he was <u>cultured</u>. Maynard is

---

[3]   Quote from the writings of Giuseppe Mazzini (1805-1872), Italian writer and revolutionary, spent time in exile in England.

back from Egypt and tells one of how he taught Arab boys the second half of Humpty Dumpty (at their special request) in the shadow of the Sphinx; and how, by moonlight, he gazed spell-bound at the gods in Karnak while from the darkness around rose the mocking voices of unimpressed Americans. Karnak[4] in the ancient Thebae; and there a queen, Hatasa, murdered her elder and was later poisoned by her younger brother whom she loved - all on a question of abstract principles: whether the old order was best, or if commerce was the road to heaven, or war - conquest - the greatest glory of the Ruler.

'A Hermit hid
In deserts of the Thebaid
Doth know these things.'[5]

I am looking forward to many things, notably bathing; also, to next August when I shall go to Budapest, and I hope yet to know some poet-people - a young Calvinist puritan[6] who writes amazingly (really epical lyrics) and others, older and therefore not so amazing (because we are just getting to something solid. - Have there ever been heard of changes as big as these modern ones?!)

As you see I am treading on air and living on moonbeams - I can't descend to earth. I feel equal to making a Psalm of praise out of a 'Select Charter' in Stubbs[7] (They are in Latin and one must know them. My Tripos is in five weeks: I have seven subjects to 'revise', most of which I have never 'mastered' at all)

Yours

F. Békássy

---

[4]   Karnak, second largest ancient religious site in the World, necropolis of Ancient Thebes.

[5]   Light-hearted reference to the poem 'The Hermit of the Thebaid' by American poet John Greenleaf Whittier (1807-1892).

[6]   Most likely Hungarian poet Gábor Oláh (1881-1942).

[7]   William Stubbs, (1825-1901) historian Bishop of Oxford, whose book, *Select Charters and other Illustrations of English Constitutional History* was part of the syllabus.

Coming back through London I picked up a Review[8] and found it full of articles by Rupert. Another paper mentioned him 'the best-known English poet of our time'. In yet another, I saw Maynard is now a Royal Commissioner (perhaps the youngest there has ever been).

They shoot up like mushrooms.

---

8   Probably *Cambridge Review.*

Letter 23 – 26 April 1913

[Cambridge]

Today [26 April 1913]

Dear Noel,

Is there anywhere, in minds as in things a substance more amazing and prefect and all-containing than *water*?! The cause of this irrelevant remark is that I have spent a day on the Upper River. But really don't you think that living water, a torrent or a duck-pound or an ocean - but even water in a glass, passes the imagination of man? A stream not only reflects its banks but is itself changed by doing so. I do love it above anything one can see. There is nothing else which makes things so beautiful except poetry and then poetry is beautiful but doesn't make other things so. (I mean it isn't the song of the nightingale that is made beautiful in Keats (Ode to it).

I went up in a Rob Roy[1] and paddled on and on and then bathed at large even half a mile of river: went on again past unknown places, new full beauties followed each other so thick that I had to stop and have lunch. Coming down one makes no noise - creatures don't notice one: herons do, but moorhen will almost let you go by before they run away over the water, and ducks, if you surprise them, will draw in their necks and painfully try to become invisible. -

That is the way I work for my Tripos! (But not always perhaps). History is a ridiculous subject, just think of doing such a lot of useless rubbish! Next year it will be better (I am learning Italian (!) to read about the Renaissance) though Political 'Science' is the most unscientific one there is.

I very much enjoyed your description of Sussex and the Grimm

---

[1] 'Rob Roy' a prototype canoe, named after the legendary Scottish hero by traveller John MacGregor, author of '*A Thousand Miles in the Rob Roy Canoe*', 1866.

story[2] with the accurate representation of Margery on the picture and I pretended to read off all the villages. The mention of Kingly Vale[3] thrilled me but you probably didn't like that expedition so much as I did, also did you see the place with <u>all</u> the foxgloves?

Such a crop of young poets in Cambridge! Four of them all on a heap - even if Luce is in Burma. I went to one of them lately and he read me <u>such</u> good poems, but only two of them, and he now publishes a lot of futile and pointless things he writes, in Cambridge papers. […]

By the way what you said about taking sides and that it was not as if all issues were already provided, was (I thought) so logical and forcible and self-evident that I was amazed (which wasn't nice of me) and wished that Mazzini might have seen it and been converted, as, to the lasting good of my soul, I have been. Also, by the way, by *semi-romanesque* I did imply that the church tower was not uniform - it is amazing just because onto the stolid, bulking base (*romanesque*) some early Humanist had put his two light and graceful towers, that also is why it is like Mark Alexander Boyd's[4] sonnet, that there isn't anything else like it. It is not however in a village but in Brunswick,[5] where the Princess goes shopping in a blue and gold Noah's Ark followed by a crowd of street-boys. - It is called St Andrewskirche.

Rupert flitted through Cambridge and picked up an MA[6]

---

[2]   One of the Grimm Brothers' (Jacob and Wilhelm) fairy-tales, *Kinder und Hausmärchen* (1812), also popular in 19th century Britain.

[3]   Nature reserve near Chichester, West Sussex.

[4]   Mark Alexander Boyd (1563-1601) Scottish poet who wrote in Latin with the exception of this one sonnet 'Fra banc to banc' written in Scots.

[5]   Braunschweig in Germany, where Békássy visited St. Andrewskirche. The reference to 'Princes' and ' Noah's Ark' is unclear.

[6]   On becoming Fellow of King's College, Cambridge in March 1913 Rupert Brooke received his MA (Master of Arts), giving him rights to eat with the other Fellows at High Table. Writing to a friend Geoffrey Fry, he says: 'You can't think how I despise you mere civilians now. *Jetzt bin ich Professor.*' (I am now a Professor) quoted in ed. Edward March *The Collected Poems of Rupert Brooke: with a Memoir.* Second edition, Sidgwick and Jackson, Ltd. London 1929, p. lxxvii,

and dined at the high table, preparing for America all the time. He has got everything requisite except the accent. He says he sees a lot of people but everybody only once a fortnight!

Also by the way, if you see James tell him he's got to come up here for some weekend!

Yours - all in a flurry-

F. Békássy

Letter 24 – 18 May 1913

King's

18 May 1913

Dear Noel,

I am now on the verge of my Trip[os], and so in a very poor way. You can imagine my condition; I came back all full of wanting to write poems and think about things, and now it is all being cut short and I am cramming - or at any rate, learning facts - almost all day, though I am not very excited about it because I know pretty well what I'll do. A day seems very long when it contains the subject-matter of a stolid history book, and the policies of kings; and so it is ages ago that we went on a Bedalian exped[ition] up the River. Lapthorn and Norah Schuster[1] came, and Pease managed it and it was all a regular success, with Pauly entertaining the company.[...]

I have often been on the river, finding that I can now work there much better than indoors, and so go out for the best part of every day. But the interruptions in my work are many, though I don't see people often. Sometimes I go for walks with a (<u>one not any</u>) poet; and then once Daphne enticed me to tea at Newnham (in their garden) - a Russian girl was there (so theatrical) so as it usually happens I talked so much that I didn't get very much out of it. I wonder how bored <u>they</u> were. That was just before Daphne went off to Hunston.

Then there is a certain Mrs Graham who looks like a Japanese lady (only not so small) and is the wife of a consul. Now she is making a book of Cambridge Verse[2] since 1900

---

[1]   Norah Schuster (1892-1991), Bedalian, eminent pathologist.

[2]   'Mrs. Graham' also known as Aelfrida Tillyard, edited *Cambridge Poets 1900-1913*, see Introduction. She married Constantine Cleanthes (Michaelides) Graham, who was Vice-Consul in Odessa from 1907 to 1910.

and wanted me to contribute, *which* (though I remember everything you said about all the bad poetry that's written) I shall do. But anyhow I've got several afternoons' enjoyment out of it, she is so charming and knows people so well.

But I am writing till things are quite over and I used never again look at my notes, and then I shall try to get out of this coil and burst into some sort of activity. I want to do lots of things but don't know what. - Is there any chance of my being able to stay at Limpsfield after term is over? (i.e. after June 10th?) Or will you be rushing off somewhere or would I be inconvenient? I suppose I shall be in England for some time before I go home, of course see Peter Watson (and the splendid Novel he is writing)[3] and Justin. Also there is Gwen and Jaques.

Sometimes to relax I read a canto of *Don Juan*,[4] or if I am very energetic (i.e. don't mind being moved) *Cyrano de Bergerac* (the one French play really worth looking at; after the Classics - such a gasconnade!)[5] People one can't always manage; if I have worked all day it is so dreadful to find them in another world from the one I want. If only people could work together! But we have done all different parts of the History and know different things.

The other day I had to manage an Anglo Chinese dinner which was very successful but only after I had had violent scenes with three chinamen on separate occasions, they were all jealous of the others making a certain speech; they hated each other for political family reasons, they were altogether beastly but very interesting to watch. I think they must all hate me by now.

What is happening with Rupert?[6]

F. Békássy

---

3   Peter Grant-Watson's novel *Where Bounds are Loosed.*
4   'Don Juan' by Byron.
5   *Cyrano de Bergerac* (1897) by Edmond Rostand.
6   Rupert Brooke left for America a week later on 21st May, having had a farewell dinner with Noel in London. He went as Overseas Correspondent of *Westminster Gazette. Song of Love*, p. 238.

I have never had an idea how <u>awful</u> people can be when they don't understand or won't listen to plain reason. There is a literary society of Sir A.T. Quiller Couch's,[7] and they talk the vaguest and the most damnable rot and <u>sickening</u> sentiment. Q included and worse than the lot. I suppose Bryn and Popham have told you all about when they were here.

[7] Sir Arthur Quiller-Couch, nickname 'Q' (1863-1944) became Professor of English Literature in 1912.

Letter 25 – 16 July 1913

Bozsok, Rohoncz, Vas vm.

16 July 1913

Dear Noel,

This is how I now live: I have breakfast - with Him[1] - at eight, in a vaulted room with oak panels. We sit in high-backed leather chairs, and talk little. It is summer, and warm. Then perhaps we go out, and then back to the library: there are many books, and bound by him in good leathers. I read the *Weltgeschichtliche Betrachtungen*[2] of the grumpy German whom Nietzsche admired but who would have nothing to do with him (Burckhardt) - or else Maupassant:[3] or *Le Breviaire des Courtisanes*[4] - which is a dialogue, or rather a story with some six characters to whom nothing happens except that they talk - Then Marie (née de Wimpffen)[5] comes in soon, and sometime during the morning I probably see the three little girls. At any rate, we are all there at dinner. It is not too hot to go out after that, and there are very many roses. I do nothing most of the day: it seems the best occupation; and it cannot be boring when one is with Them.

Of course one talks, but not much, being a little chastened. - During the first days, he *showed* me some of his writings; and then once Marie opened a mysterious cupboard which is part of a bookshelf, and there were little manuscript volumes bound in vellum, and she made me look at etchings or poems or little bits of writing - but only the things which profane eyes were allowed to see because the rest belongs only to the two of them.

---

[1]   Gyula Verebi Végh.
[2]   'Reflections on World Literature' by Jacob Burckhardt (1818-1897) Swiss art historian.
[3]   Guy de Maupassant, French writer (1815-1893).
[4]   `The Courtesans' Breviary' by Jean Puget de la Serre (1594-1665).
[5]   Wife of Gyula Verebi Végh.

There are woods to walk in, and supper by the light of candles with yellow shades. There is nothing in the house that does not enter into their lives. There are warm evenings full of moonshine and white roses. You see I am staying for a week with these people. I have told you about them: he is my cousin twice removed, but about forty, a humanist - artist - gentleman - Nietzschean: his wife is the daughter of a sometime Consul at Rome. [...]

So at last there is more placidity. Of course I *did* like London very much (I don't mean *you* but only the others) it was full of rare pleasures. It *is* a very agreeable sort of way to live. It would annoy you if I write about the different times I was with you, and of course there is nothing to be said about them; except that I don't know if you imagine how good it sometimes was. If not, please do so.

What it is, to be with real people! - Yesterday evening I had a long talk with Marie, ostensibly about my sister; but as I was thinking of M[argery] all the time, the result was that I know she is among the very best people I know, and the kindest.

[...]

I have thought about the Necessity for War (now that all the able men of Bulgaria are being killed off)[6] or how the most important thing for art is its subject (its theme) because it is like a god to whom the art is an altar, so that the value of the art will (indirectly) be determined by its value - for instance Medieval Art was about a God, who inspired it). Of course I admit that looking at a finished work, its subject does not in the smallest degree matter to its value. By all means, paint potatoes. But the subject of the whole art matters to the painter and therefore in practice to any picture he paints. *L'Art pour l'art* is gibberish, and that to make great works is enough to be a good artist is a piece of insolence.

You see I can't talk about ordinary things. I wonder whether

I have just stepped aside for a short interval, leaving myself to be continued in a next instalment, or whether this is a crisis.

However I wish I had seen you later. Also I hope this letter won't get you just before your exams, which must be some time now. The letter you sent to Brunswick Square[6] got me when I was so 'aufgeregt'[7] that for the moment it was all but wasted. (By the way, tell me about triple-souled water. Why triple? I have got a reason, but it is not very solid). - I also and in a less degree wish I had managed to see Peter and Justin. But they are probably as well off without me, and I really can't complain, so much - in the way of feelings at any rate, and of all sorts of experience - has happened with me since the Tripos. This, as everything else is of course ultimately due to you - but then there is no need to think about that. I don't, just now.

Yours
F. Békássy

I wonder if I thanked people enough, e.g. Bryn - but perhaps they know that I assume that they realise that I was in raptures about the more important things e.g. food and sleeping and talking.

---

6   London residence of John Maynard Keynes
7   excited, nervous (German)

Letter 26 – 15 August 1913

Kis Sennye, Rum, Vm

15 August 1913

Dear Noel,

Why don't you write? And I have so much to say! Is it on purpose or by chance? If it is on purpose, at any rate tell me the reason (the real reason).

Sei - Zwischen uns - at least - *Wahrheit!*[1] (If it isn't a sin to quote a classic)

Yours
F. Békássy

Of course perhaps it is only chance, but how am I to know? Or do I only get letters when you are especially sorry for me, or if I behave as I ought?! (Don't be offended)

---

[1]   'Let there be truth between us' (German), from 'Iphigenia in Tauris' (1787) play by Johann Wolfgang Goethe.

Letter 27 − 5 September 1913

[Ó-Barok]¹

5 September 1913

Dear Noel,

You make me want to find excuses for myself (though there aren't any; I'm just like that;) - I wish I could answer with a letter like yours.

I am writing from Barok⁻ which is where Flora lives and where I haven't been oh for ten years perhaps. She is very different (grown up; at her ease; not awkward) but I am more selfish than usually, not caring what people are like as long as they trouble, and don't trouble too much, about me. She read me her novel ('*Dies Veneris*') and of course she is seriously a writer. I like the book very much; it is so full of naturalness; and its people's feelings are so sensibly managed (e.g. they feel all sorts of things: and it doesn't very much influence what happens to their lives and relations. - As you said, about people in general) Not qualities one would expect in a first novel, written *aet.* [age] 19!

I fled from Sennye. Since I came away from among the roses I have been having headaches every day. It is very humiliating and I haven't even been ill, but couldn't do anything. I enjoyed life (in the intervals, i.e. from 11 a.m. to 2 p.m.) and then some few days it was hot and I bathed all along my river; struggling, being carried down stream and roasting on the sand. I found a book of dull stories - Hewlett² - but about fairies. H. is a well-to-do and sentimental Englishman with a bald head, but he has a good idea of what fairies mean, though

---

¹ Barok or Ó-Barok, village where Békássy's cousin Flóra lived.
² *The Forest Lovers*, a romance of medieval times by Maurice Henry Hewlétt (1861-1923) published in 1898.

he makes them look ridiculous. It's one of the books Tonika reads - there are perhaps two dozen; excluding anything she doesn't really want to read.

Flora has two small brothers, and her mother is in all the feminist movements, a thin, masculine, sensitive lady, but not fanatic; she knows what to do with people, and knows them. I am more sure they see me from two sides here than anywhere else.

The summer is just beginning; it is as hot as the first days of August ought to be. The country is grand: wide plateau-land ending in a steep ridge of dolomites; straggling woods; maize; stage; half-downy hills. And clean tones, and sunsets!

My excuse for coming here was literary, I said I wanted some articles in old papers and so I came to Budapest. (This is near.) I was only one day there; one day has followed the other since then, and I am continuing to waste marketable years (I haven't had a history book in my hands since June) and am proud because I shall soon write big words about Hungarian literature;[3] and am behaving in as Dr. Johnsonish[4] a way as I can, arguing with the persuasiveness of an ox (we get on with Flora as though we had always seen each other. This, I may say, is her merit.) Eating, sleeping, and not at all ashamed of myself, but I was very uneasy when I had to unpack my poems and read - they are high-flown. I don't know which leg to stand on when I am confronted with then.

I envy you all your camps and everything else. Zilliacus was at the O.B. meeting? You may be in Scotland now, with - Lytton[5]. But no, you sent Lytton off on a continental tour: I met him in Budapest. He was in a splendid car, had a thick cigar in his mouth, and waved to me. (Tall, red-bearded, *distingué*;

---

[3] Reference to the essay mentioned in the Introduction, the English version of
     which was not published.

[4] Dr Samuel Johnson (1709-1784) author of the *Dictionary of the English Language.*

[5] Lytton Strachey, see Main Characters.

spanish cape, earrings, oyster-eyes - is there a genus of Lyttons scattered over the earth?)

I am full of enthusiasm really, about Hungarian writers - but I wouldn't own up to it here. Literature is such a queer thing with us. I am sick of English writings; I hate the Teutonic habit of being overpowered by life. The only books I can for the time being think about, are French; they are splendid people, who can smoke *'une cigarette sur le Golgotha (on bien l'Olympe) en contemplant quelque couchant aux tous inédits*[6] - although it is true that in the end they become Roman Catholics.

And now I have to read Jane Austen. *Emma.*[7] It is a wretched thing to be doing. <u>Why</u> do people tolerate her? Full of virtues and wit, of course, but!!! -

Altogether I think I have been just as much asleep as anyone, all this year (only I dream violently) I have lucid intervals - as now - but now I am disgusted with people; and can't bear to think of their lives - they are not decent. But then my feelings change such a lot, it isn't worth while remembering them all.

- My various regards to the people whom I don't find disgusting even at 10 p.m. (now) which is the lowest point.

Yours
F. Békássy

I left Sennye a place of desolation. After I got and before I read your letter there was a hailstorm. The hail that fell was an inch and a half across. It lasted for ten minutes. All the windows were smashed in the first minute, like a fusillade - The roof slipped down some inches each side leaving a wide crack at the

---

[6]   [Smoke] 'a cigarette on Golgotha, while contemplating the setting sun in its unique colours.'. Quote from a letter by Jules Laforgue (1860-1887). Békássy inserts a joking reference to Mount Olympus.
[7]   Jane Austen (1775-1817). Her novel *Emma*, was published in 1815.

ridge - men working in the fields were carried home in litters afterwards. Trees were left leafless with their bark hanging in strips. The ground was covered with torn leaves, fruit, tiles, wreckage - it all sounds melodramatic and was horrible and left me indignant, and bewildered.

Letter 28 – 4 October 1913

4 October 1913
(I've been away and only got your letter today)[1]

My dear Noel,

No, no! It will almost do, but not quite. Since your last letter before this, I have had plenty of time to think. I was thinking that my last year in Cambridge would be quiet; that I would not, (I hoped), see you very soon, but later on, towards the winter.

Now I get your letter, and laugh at your feeling more and more tied up as time goes on; and disapprove of the way you speak of my behaving 'wonderfully' etc.

'Conversations are the thing we've *always Both* enjoyed'? - at Bedales. Afterwards, what *I* enjoyed, was *you*.

As for my behaving well, the only alternative would be to try for adventure in the medieval or tyranny in the Renaissance style! However, it is *always* more natural for me, *not* to try to influence anyone in any way, but to enjoy whatever of actual relations, as they already are, are enjoyable. (I am beginning to realise this and to smile at myself for having pretended the opposite).

But it will not quite do for me not to see you; it isn't fair. You must do as I have done; behave! - and not get tied up into knots: because you know that it is worthwhile for us to see each other. - (How could you think that I didn't notice your scared and tied-upness?) - the lopsidedness does not exist; only a certain amount of constraint of different kinds on *both* sides, - which, mon Dieu, isn't such a serious ~~affair~~ - matter.

And for pity's sake! Do not relegate our acquaintance to the writing of literary letters! - Surely there are many people now,

---

[1] Békássy had been staying with his cousin Flora. See previous letter.

with whom you can talk as well? I suppose you like writing letters, though. (of course I would like to get yours when you write of my country with its vigorous mothers and devastating storms, but I could manage without!) - I hope I am not hurting you, in my turn. By the way, what an idea, that by and at our meetings you can *possibly* hurt me, as long as you are *not* afraid of doing so.

You see, you can go on with whatever your line is - I wish I knew *what* it was - and I too seem to have found a way now for myself. However, although we have no intentions of having anything to do with each other and our respective business, we can show some amount of intelligent curiosity towards each other's doings and 'beings' - i.e. we can enjoy meeting and seeing what we are each about. *That* isn't lopsided?

F. Békássy

'Beautiful' James [Strachey] - this makes me jealous - a little. But you are right that my headaches are unsuitable.

I am glad you wrote first; I can only make sparks like an anvil.

You think lives dreary? But no! Not with so many people for each to be with?

On 4 January 1914 Noel was to write to Rupert Brooke about trying to break off her relationship with Békássy: 'I [in the autumn] - in my zeal - tried to induce Békássy to become a stranger [...]. But he pointed out that it was nonsense and would be unfair and I agreed. We saw him in Cambridge when D[aphne] and I went up one week-end [...]. And he was wonderfully nice. He entertained in his continental room, so empty and tall; and rode and talked; I thought he was probably superior to anyone I knew.' Song of Love, p. 260

Letter 29 – 1 November 1913

King's College Cambridge

Sunday, 1 November 1913

Dear Noel,

It is now three weeks since I came back, and this year is really proving very strange! I hardly know where to begin describing the term, everything is so different.

You know Peter Watson was here for ten days, finishing his novel (I read it and found it good: it is full of lust and murder and the survivors live happily ever afterwards.) Of course I saw so much of him that I didn't do anything else. He was in high spirits - just think, feeling certain one had found one's own job -; his book has been taken by Duckworth's and taken up by Conrad.[1] The last I had seen of him was in Switzerland last January: but I must have been very intolerable at that time.

However, I had determined to lead a continent life this year: working and only seeing people when they came to see me. I did go to the Jaques' of course, and we picked blackberries

---

[1]   The novel *Where Bonds Are Loosed* on which Peter Grant-Watson is working, was mentioned in an earlier letter (18 May 1913). Joseph Conrad (1857-1924) Polish-born English writer took Grant-Watson under his wings and recommended the book to Duckworth Publishers, who published it in 1914.

and I saw J[aques]'s Christ on the Cross, and that too is very good. I am finding such a lot of my friends' things are good! I mean really good, worthy, eternal, etc. There is Luce for instance - and he may be coming back in December, almost before Rupert!

Yesterday I even went to the Cornford's - (you must remember them) She had a baby - a girl - Helena - six weeks ago; and it has made them both different: more vivacious and bright. (Cornford is usually so - vacuous.) This time they were talking hard to each other all the time, very evidently enjoying it. But I was buried behind my spectacles and everything seemed very dim. You see I have only worn them for two days, and they make me look like a Chinese judge, and I feel old, old, very old in them. Bliss and Raisley also say I look like a woman, like Mr Rice (!) or like Mr Sedgwick of Trinity[2] (a worm - you don't know him) and many other unpleasant things .

Many other things have happened: I go to Dickinson for Essays and yesterday I rode with him among the brilliant colours of which Cambridge landscapes are full now - for the trees are keeping their leaves and beeches are very red, and the sunshine very bright. Then - what lots of people one does meet, all the same - I met an Armenian I know (Altounyan)[3] who is just back from Turkey (not in Europe, but Asia - Aleppo.) He is thin and brown and consumed with fire, and very modest and very amazing; he told me a Splendid thing, how the Oxford men who were excavating at Aleppo (Hittite remains, <u>very</u> old) <u>use</u> the amazing earthenware they find; - and <u>when a piece breaks</u> they send it to the British Museum! It's a great thing that enthusiasts have no respect for museums and other rubbish-heaps.

---

[2]   Leon Rice, famous tenor of Trinity College Chapel and Adam Sedgwick, tutor at Trinity College, Cambridge.

[3]   Dr Ernest H.R. Altounyan (1889-1962) medical doctor and poet of Irish-Armenian origin. After Cambridge he married and settled down in the Lake District.

My eyes have been useless till now - by the way all my headaches were about them and will now stop - but now I am doing work. I sit in a deep armchair and put a standing light on its wooden arm; the fire is in front of me and a plate of apples on the windowsill. Then I gaze at a page of black and white design until it yields its idea. - It is an astonishing process, work.

Besides work, there are of course 'activities'. I must read a paper on the Balkans and another on Samuel Butler[4] and then I am desperately trying to publish an article; and this week a very unsavoury book is coming out - a Cambridge Anthology with a preface by Q (Sir Arthur Quiller-Couch.) and pages of slop and sentiment by a dreadful Mrs. Graham[5] whose Christian name is Aelfrida (with an ae!); and I am in it too. So everything is full of disquiet.

I am sorry Daphne is no longer at Newnham - not that I saw very much of her, but still it makes a difference.[...]

I wonder why I feel much more certain of myself than I used to - there is no reason: I don't know what I'll do, I don't even know if I shall write (I mean really write: i.e. write everything I have) but I seem all right anyhow. And - I am shaking off one after another, the shackles which bind me to England. I shall not mind when I go. (That will be next July, I must serve my year in the army: so to the wall go all plans about a 4th year at King's, about Classics, etc.) And though I still say to myself that I shall soon come back to England, I know it can't be true.

But I am careful not to tell this to anyone, because I must at least get all I can from the present and not let people get the idea that I am passing and do not matter much: just think!

---

[4] Békássy wrote an essay on the Balkans and one on *The Note-Books of Samuel Butler* (1912). Though the one on the Balkans has been lost, a Hungarian version of the latter survived, see: Sennyey Weiner, pp. 258-63.

[5] Békássy had obviously changed his good opinion of Aelfrida Tillyard (Mrs. Graham).

if James knew, he would think me a butterfly (how wrongly!) and the other people would give me up for dead before I really was: and I don't even want to write my testament, but somehow muddle through things and come out at the other end.

I believe for a time I shall go away altogether into unheard-of parts, where to 'men whose heads' as good as 'grow beneath their shoulders'[6] for all that I can get out of them - *'mais l'avenir est sur les genoux des Dieux.'*[7]

If I were as modest as Altounyan I would have thought of witty stories to write, or at any rate have written about other things than myself - but then!

My reading has become so enthusiastically specialised (in themes) and universal (in scope) that it is hard to speak of it. In my essay on Miss Austen[8] I made a long simile (of which I was proud) concerning Chess: where (as in her novels) the interest is in the game: The game is governed by the Characters of the Pieces, and their points of view: the Knight moves along the side of imaginary triangles; to the Queen the board is a Japanese sun with straight rays. - but it does not matter to the game, whether the pieces are carved or smooth, or made of ivory or wood. You see I think Miss Austen does not really describe characters.

I was in London for an afternoon when I came back here (but so Hungarian still, that I could hardly speak English); but I didn't manage to go and see Bryn. How are they?

Yours
F. Békássy

---

[6]   Quote from Shakespeare's *Othello* , Act I Scene 3, lines 168-169.
[7]   'But the future lies in the lap of the Gods', a quote from Homer's *Odyssey*, which Békássy must have read in an essay by French writer Dugas Montbel, published in 1830.
[8]   Jane Austen.

Have you heard anything more about the Omega workshops?[9]
When I came, they seemed altogether gone to pieces.

---

[9] The Omega Workshop was established in 1913 by the artist Roger Fry (1866-1934), a member of the Bloomsbury Group. It enabled artists to have a steady income, by working in the workshop for three and a half days at 7s 6d (37p), designing furniture, mosaics and a range of objects for the home in bold colours. The pieces were not signed with individual names, but with the workshop's symbol the Greek letter Ω. In 1910 Fry organised an exhibition in London, *Manet and the Post-Impressionists*, a term which he coined.

Letter 30 – 26 November 1913

King's College Cambridge

26 November 1913

Dear Noel,

I was in London yesterday and today, and heard from Bryn that you were coming up, but had not got your letter. When I went round to (19) Marlboro'[1] no one was there and I left a hurried note. If you care for a ride - by the way I suppose you both ride - it may stand; but anyhow come to lunch at 1.15.

I went to town because of my eyes. I in spectacles! Of course it was impossible. I don't have to wear them, it was all a mistake. I heard from Bryn all about Bubbles (J. Macartney Robbins)[2] - in fact all about most things. I was there yesterday evening and talked a lot and bored them both.

I like your Mrs. Dryhurst,[3] taken in conjunction with those people at the Larkin[4] meeting. It must have been good to see- I have once been in a crowd but that was <u>threatening</u> (it was at Budapest) and they weren't intelligent beings.

[…]

I must send this tonight- that note must have seemed absurd - it is after 12 and I travelled with a number of knuts.[5]

Yours

F. Békássy

---

[1]   St. John's Wood, London, where Noel lived during term-time while at University.

[2]   Old Bedalian.

[3]   Nannie Florence Dryhurst (1856-1930) suffragette.

[4]   James Larkin, (1876-1947) trade union activist, one of the founders of the Irish Labour Party. He coined the phrase 'A fair day's pay for a fair day's work'. As one of the leaders of the strike in Dublin, which brought the city to a halt (The Dublin Lockout), he made a speech in Manchester's Free Trade Hall on 16th November 1916 to gain support. The hall was packed and thousands gathered in the streets outside.

[5]   Obsolete slang word for playboy, dandy.

Letter 31 – 11 January 1914

Szombathely

[11th January 1914]

Dear Noel,

I am sorry I didn't see you when I came through London - I only saw Adrian (because he is good to be with) and James[1] (because he said he was going away.) Now there is lots to write: and the best thing that has happened is that I needn't have ANY MORE HEADACHES

[...]

I am quite alone now for three days, in the middle of a great desert of a town where I know nobody and can't go out. It is a big house and all the rooms silent, with empty chairs everywhere [...] I had tea, and saw all the empty chairs, and filled them all with people - each sitting where I thought he would in reality choose to sit. There was Moore[2], on a sofa, and McCarthy[3], and Lytton stroking his beard, in a high-backed wooden chair with the window behind him, then Maynard (next to McCarthy then a Mr Felkin, and so reaching to another circle where Sheppard[4] sprawled on a divan, and by the little round table with the tea sat I and (of all people) Moore's brother, the poet[5]: and opposite me with his back

---

[1]   Adrian Stephen (1883-1948) brother of Virginia Woolf, member of the Bloomsbury Group. James Strachey, (see Main Characters), soon afterwards left for Moscow, a Mecca in those days for theatre and ballet, (H.G. Wells and actor/theatre manager H. Granville-Barker also visited around the same time). On his way home he visited the major theatre companies in several European cities including Budapest. See Hale, *Friends and Apostles*, pp. 276-277.

[2]   G.E. Moore, see Main Characters.

[3]   Desmond MacCarthy (1877-1952) literary critic.

[4]   John Tresidder Sheppard (1881-1968), Fellow, later Provost of King's College, Cambridge 1933-1954. A letter to him from Békássy is included in this volume.

[5]   Thomas Sturge Moore (1870-1944) brother of G.E. Moore. Several of his poems were included in the anthology *Georgian Poetry* (1912) ed. Edward Marsh.

to the other circle, fidgeting on a small uncomfortable chair, Dickinson in his riding-things; Stokoe[6] (whom you met) listening to Sturge Moore, opposite him, but rather far away, and half hidden by the big back of a chair; and then there was quite another circle, to my left; Bliss, rather heated, and talking a lot, in a chair against the wall; two other people on a long stool, slanting away opposite him; one of them, a very nice young man, who smiles and is amused, to whom he was talking; the other, who sat further away and smoked and didn't talk, was the cause of Bliss being there at all, finally Uncle Raisley, on the further side of the stove (this circle was loosely round the stove) in what is probably the most comfortable chair of all. I could see out of the corner of my eye how he sat with his arms crossed, and I smiled.

Well, but I must pull myself together if this is to be a letter at all! - I was going to say, I am now enjoying the loneliness and wouldn't for the world see anyone. I am fairly idle; not that I haven't enough to do! All my work; and then books - I am reading 'Jerusalem' (Lagerlöf)[7] and because it is very full of fantasies and imagination, I like it; but its fantasy-making isn't quite satisfying, perhaps because it is less serious than, say, Dostoevsky (I am thinking of the story Myshkin[8] tells, about his Swiss village and about Christian virtue.)

[…]

I am really very tired and look forward in terror to the amount of work I now know I shall do till June. It will be no use. I can't get a first. If I could, I would have got a II/1 last time. My being alone is because my people have gone up to Budapest, my great aunt has died, quite suddenly, and I am not going to her funeral. I

---

[6]   Frank W. Stokoe see Introduction.

[7]   'Jerusalem', novel by Selma Lagerlöf (1858-1940) Swedish writer, the first woman to win the Nobel Prize for Literature,1909.

[8]   The hero of *The Idiot*, novel by Fyodor Dostoevsky (1821-1881).

thought funerals were absurd, but as a matter of fact they aren't. I shall be in London on Saturday, I think, and if I go to Marlboro' Rd in the afternoon, will I find anyone there? But perhaps you aren't in town yet. I wonder has James really gone? - [...] I am very lenient just now but it's true: it doesn't do to have your mind full of things [...] That is like books, of course, and one of the things I care for about them is that I should get something out of them which is good to think about when I like. That is how I don't like Jane Austen (about whom you said something to the same effect, about the taste it left in one's mouth.)

To return - for instance it doesn't do, does it, to think about Jaques? So you see it isn't quite in proportion with my likes and dislikes. Of course it can't be, because if I were to go altogether on the principle of mine, I would be merely considering the future, or the past: and I am not so impractical. *'Cueillez des aujourd'hui'*[9]...etc. I mean I like Jaques, altogether, not only to be with. I went there on the last day of term, and it was so far (and good!) that I couldn't come back, and so stayed the night. - Where does Baines[10] live?

Now shall I give an account of my life since the end of term?

1. Petersfield, with Mrs Jarry.[11] That was to see my sisters, not all the cardboard boxes with people inside and things going on inside them, and myself disconsolately walking about outside (I mean Bedales). Of course everyone at the school was nice, to ME poor Stranger!

2. Hellerau![12] (It sounds like an exclamation of joy, halfway between Heurekal! and Halleluja!) But you must ask Marjorie

9   'pick today [your roses of life]'last line of 'Sonnet pour Hélène', by French Renaissance poet Pierre de Ronsard. (1524-1585).
10   Most probably Helton Godwin Baynes (1882-1943) M.D., analytical psychologist, whom Noel must have mentioned in her previous letter. He later became Jung's assistant and translator.
11   Nadine Jarintzoff.
12   A district of Dresden, the first garden city in Germany founded in 1909. Its annual arts festival (banned later by the Nazis) attracted visitors from all over Europe.

Strachey[13] about that. I stayed four days and it was very good. She can be just as nice as she can be nasty and she is always one or the other.

3. Then I was at home, which meant Christmas, and Tonika and her husband, and all this strange, silent and perhaps dull family, which is WE, all so different and really all very fine, I think. (It was a pity we were in the town.) I say we are strange because we take everything for granted and talk so little about things. - Then Tonika went, and my brothers went lately bit by bit.

4. When one (that is, I) meets a very charming young lady, does one talk about what one thinks, to you? She is quite young and has brown hair and was brought up in a Convent and I met her two years ago, when we had quite a flirtation (and nobody guessed) which came to an end soon. She is good, sensible, and very natural. I love to imagine her as she is at home, rather wild and rather easy. I met her again the other day, and at the time I just thought she was more sensible than the rest. That I liked to hear what she had to say, and that was all. (But I came home in the evening and just lay down on my bed and sobbed; so I think that it must have been more than that and that I have that pleasure in the totality of her appearance and voice and manner etc.) which ... but I know that it isn't at all really love (and so can write about it.) But then I must explain that I have violent desires it is true, but only when and in proportion as I also like, and have no desire where I have no affection.

[...]

Now really, but one doesn't talk about this to you! What have I been writing? I didn't mean to and I don't know why I've written just as though I were writing in a diary - please don't

---

[13] Marjorie Strachey, Lytton Strachey's younger sister, writer and teacher.

try to find anything in this that isn't there; it's all down in ink, and there is nothing between the letters!

5. We've sometimes gone out to Sennye to skate or shoot. It is always romantic and I like that though not the shooting. It is all woods and open bosky meadows, now white, looking like a fairy-story-book illustration, with the wild geese flying in the purple air, and a sunset going on (Third Act) and the light changing, and such colours! In the dark evening we drive to the station; we have locked up the big, solitary, thick-walled house, in one room of which a fire is still burning in the open fireplace .... Isn't that romantic?

However, I don't mind going back to England; and now I shall get up and go out, and then do some work. I am reading about the Italian Renaissance and in some of it there is (although I like the whole affair) something quite crooked and insane: Férrante, King of Naples,[14] collects mummies made out of the bodies of the enemies he murdered; and dies of a bad conscience; and so on.

This is the longest letter I've written. I hope you can get through it. I am anxious to hear news of all sorts, whether Gerald Shove has got his fellowship, whether Rupert is back from Tahiti and Luce from Burma,[15] with or without a wife. I shall know in a week's time.

Yours
F. Békássy

---

[14] Ferdinand I, King of Naples (1423-1494). His strange exploits were related by Jacob Burckhardt in his book *Die Kultur der Renaissance in Italien* (1860).
[15] Gerald Shove did not get his Fellowship in King's. (He received it only in 1926). Rupert Brooke came back to England only a few months later. Gordon Luce also came back but returned to Burma where he lived until 1964.

Letter 32 – 10 February 1914

[Cambridge]

10 February 1914

Dear Noel,

I wish you would write some time, - I can't write a decent letter, being full of work and not altogether well. Besides, I wrote a long letter from Hungary.

Cambridge is not very full of fun, but I am enjoying it. Today especially has been a good day. I have just come from a long talk with Moore, which is one of the good things of life. I always feel that I am headstrong, vague, lenient, and full of 'Ahnung '[1] so that only a few threads keep me to Reason. Now Moore is so splendid that I can talk to him only if I try to be, as every good man should, reasonable in what I say; and yet we talk about all the things most ingrained in me!

Before that, I was out in a Rob Roy on the upper river. I meant to go alone, but met Lucas[2], also in one. Lucas is the name of a Trinity man in his first year. I like this about him, that he has all the humanities - I suppose I mean decent disinterested feelings -, and admire him because he is sensible; that is to say, clear and honest, in thinking. And I like him - it is always best to say, for no reason, just evidently. So we get on. But being on the river was good besides: you know what I think about water: 'the stubbornness of smooth still water-masses' and all that.

In the morning, when I do most of my work, I managed to get up interest in Charles V[3], the Man with too many dominions; Emperor in Germany and of the World; King of Spain, Ruler

---

[1] foreboding (German).

[2] Frank Laurence (Peter) Lucas (1894-1967) see Main Characters.

[3] Charles V. Holy Roman Emperor (1500-1558).

of Sicily, Naples and Africa, and of the Netherlands; who exasperated all because he was not Omnipresent, and needed Omnipresence because he couldn't imagine things from a distance - but of course I must read of all the marriages and treaties: Chiévres, Gattinara, Luaysa, Cobos - just names -, of Pope and Prince and Heretic; so you have fact crowding on fact, and it is only if I am wide awake or lucky, that

'... from its black and white design, the page
Sullenly yields its ponderous adage.
And from all fancies disengaged, there stands
The essential concept. ...'[4]

I suppose, however, I shouldn't quote poetry, unless it be Shakespeare (or, Lucas would say, Tennyson[5] - a queer idea of his)

I find it lucky that for Essays I go to Dickinson. He is so forbearing. You see, what happens when I write Essays is this: I begin with a bold sentence, stating what I conceive the bottom fact in the subject, or the necessary first assumption. But then I think it needs modification. I modify; then modify the modification; then think 'but on the other hand', then ... you can imagine what happens to the essay.

This, they say, is my poetic nature: and they explain that poets are nervous young men, who begin to write down what they want to say, but then comes a word ending in the same way as one they've already written; surprised at this, they are flurried and upset, and begin all over again saying the same thing. -

Is there anything else to tell? Maynard? Raisley? Riding? Dickinson's discussion - society? Music? - Art - Bliss has a grand old Brewery in which he paints the scenery for the Marlowe play (the Alchymist)[6]: it is high up over a large yard,

---

[4] Unidentified quotation.
[5] Alfred, Lord Tennyson (1809-1892) Poet Laureate.
[6] *The Alchemist*, play by Ben Jonson (1572-1637) being performed at the Marlowe Society.

and if one goes and shouts to him, he comes out onto a narrow, railed platform, and, with the sky and the blackness of the open doorway behind him, acts you a speech - Danton[7] preferably, of his own imagined Pathos and Melodrama. It is very high up: no steps lead to it and in a cloudy sky the thing is thrilling to watch.

I must work - the secret of life says, Maynard, is a 12 hours sleep.

Yours
F. Békássy

I saw Jaques - he is painting and thinks he can after all do it. He gave me a book, which when I read I went to sleep. It made me dream symbolical dreams. Gwen thinks I am becoming more and more Hungarian, and gave me a thorough luncheon when I arrived ravenous. I thought that they were getting on and well. How is Bryn?

---

[7] Georges Danton (1759-1794) French revolutionary.

Letter 33 – 7 April 1914

[Kis-Sennye]

Wednesday Evening[1]
[7 April 1914]

Dear Noel,

This must be something like the eighth letter I've begun, to try to answer yours, but I couldn't do it before I came home. I was so all to pieces, I am amazed now to think how I was drifting! and now that I have pulled myself together, I have so many things to do and to think about.

I had better say at once that it is very late and so - however, we shall see what happens.

I've been very happy and contented here. A big house with 12 people - all sitting round a large table at supper, Father at one end and Mother at the other, and we all in between, all very different and getting more and more different from each other! At present, however, just as we get more different we also have more and more to do with each other (that's like my idea of history - increase of variation <u>and</u> inter-communication.) Besides, you know, it is Easter, and Tonika and her husband are here, and everyone is feeling this ought to be something of an occasion.

Today I've hardly had my clothes on, all the morning I've bathed 'running wild', all over the river (because it is hot here, with all the proper attributes for April): all the afternoon we all bathed, in a more civilised way, and had a great fight with sand and mud; and half the evening I've been out in the

---

[1]   The letter is undated, the postmark is unclear, but as it is written on a
    Wednesday and it being Easter, the date must be April 7. The year must be 1914,
    as in the letter Békássy mentions his sister Antonia's husband whom she married
    in the autumn of 1913.

woods. It's rather queer the way one gets with one's brothers and sisters, so that one never talks about anything except in a very few words, and it is nevertheless agreed that one knows all about each other; and besides, one has fits of suddenly liking them more than before. It's so easy, too, to get onto good terms with them - no talking necessary: it just happens that one goes out fishing, or discusses how maps can be made (projections) or how one could live if one had to manage, suddenly, without any civilised thing: or, if instead of being all scattered and learning and making careers, we were all to stop here and work on the land and each learn a different job - bees, fruit, dairy, swine, etc.! And there it is. (We used always to smoke a peace-pipe when this happened, but the 'tobacco'- dried walnut leaves - tasted so bad that we gave it up, and besides, one couldn't really go on doing it; but it doesn't matter much).

I feel I am something like myself again (- after all this time!) with the proper confidence in everything, and the sanity that one <u>tends</u> (!) to lose when one is trying hard to be influenced by every casual thing one meets. [...]

I've just found a whole packet of my grandfather's[2] writings. They are rather sad to see. First, a lot of things about books - I suppose people would call them reviews but they're not like that because he only wrote them for himself [...] Then there are short stories, plays, a novel, all sorts of notes; about Jews, about Credit, about Astronomy, etc. etc. but all the stories etc. are only a page, or - a half a page, and break off before one can guess what would have happened; and the novel is just one very exciting scene, and a preface saying novels shouldn't be like Werther.[3][...]

---

[2]   Elek Bezerédj, Békássy's maternal grandfather.
[3]   *The Sorrows of Young Werther*, sentimental novel by Johann Wolfgang Goethe, in which the hero takes his own life, creating a spate of copycat suicides.

If I begin to tell you about all that happened in England before I came here, I shall get altogether involved and muddled. It's just a mass of impressions under which I writhed and wriggled and wished I were out of it all. I'm <u>not</u> a fast liver! However, it was just 'an enchantment', and I've 'woken up to reality' - how ridiculously people use these! Obviously the enchantment must be disquieting and make one uneasy, and the reality must settle everything.

Although haven't <u>written</u> anything, I know that I could - if I had anything to write about, so I am even proud, and at any rate certain that I shall write poetry - or whatever it's going to be, something good. I am so sure that for anything really good, a 'knack' is quite insufficient - a knack of being able to tell things, or an eye for things that will tell (say in a description of a personality.) It seems absurd if you put it the other way i.e. that what a poet must have is not, a special ability for writing verse - but it's true; the thing he must have is much more all-round and takes up all of him, and if he has it, he will bend the words to his will after a time, in some may - it may be a queer way. Unless some other material suits him better. [...]

By the way, I didn't know him. [his Grandfather]

I am coming back to England on Friday, and shall be in London on Sunday next. But of course you will be at Limpsfield?

I haven't seen you for ever so long. I don't count the time you came to Cambridge (when Justin was there) and won't even mention the time after that (Piccadilly Circus, or wherever it was!) - By the way I hope you're not still thinking about that letter I wrote in the autumn when you said you didn't think it was any good our meeting (!) but only the letters were some use(!) etc.

And I do think, too, it isn't quite fair about letters, either. You write so much news about everyone, and don't really stick to your arrangement about writing about yourself at all, while here am I, writing all these mad letters of various sorts about myself.

Please, don't mind all this. I wonder whether you like getting a letter like this, and what on earth you can like about it, if you do.

I'm very vague, and my mind's all to pieces.

F. Békássy

I hope Bryn and Margery didn't mind my going away without saying anything? I thought perhaps they wouldn't mind.

Letter 34 – 30 April 1914

[Cambridge]

Thursday, 30 April, 1914

Dear Noel,

Your letter came today (it was sent home while I was with Maynard in Asheham.)[1] I can't yet get over not having come in time for Sunday, but I thought perhaps you wouldn't want me to come in the middle of the week, and so went to Asheham.

From there one can see Ash Down and guess at Limpsfield. It was quiet and lovely.

I like my work less than anything in the world now. But the Term will be splendid. Peter (Watson) is coming up and staying at the Vicarage. (Grantchester) so that he will make the third association it has for me. The first was Rupert (when I first got to know him), the second a Quaker[2] I know.

I am going to meet my sisters when they come and pack them off to Bedales. That, I think is tomorrow week. (Isn't it?) Can I come down to Limpsfield some time that weekend? By the way, have you seen Peter's book[3] yet? Read it and tell people what you think of it. I think Brunswick Square will pooh-pooh him, but only because they are prejudiced - But I forgot, Justin is there nowadays. Tonight (with Peter) I am going to the Cornfords. Frances has just lately read a 'chit-chat

---

[1]   Maynard Keynes was renting Asheham House, Firle, Sussex from Leonard and Virginia Woolf while they were away. Békássy wrote his sonnet (included in this volume) 'I am that bondsman whom an earthly grace…'while staying there. Later in July it appears that Békássy visited again and became closer to the painter Duncan Grant, ex-lover of Maynard Keynes. They hoped to meet in Vienna for Christmas, but the outbreak of war prevented this. Frances Spalding, *Duncan Grant*, Chatto & Windus (1997) p. 154.

[2]   Clive Carey (1883-1968) Rupert Brooke's old singing teacher. In 1945 he was appointed Director of Opera at Sadler's Wells, c.f. *Song of Love* pp. 271-3.

[3]   Peter Grant-Watson.

epic' of mine, and liked it, and has still got it. But then we had a violent correspondence because she said it made her sick to think of two men falling in love with each other! Which, I said, was absurd, and due to a misconception.

Harold[4] (can I forget a man with whom I wrestled ?) I quite agree, either extremely wise (having everything before them) or quite foolish, but the first is, I think, more likely!

There is a great deal of news, but I hope anyhow I shall see you in a week's time? - If one always works when one is meant to, there is plenty of time.

Yours,
F. Békássy
[...]

---

[4]   Harold Hobson (1891-1973) neighbour of the Oliviers in Limpsfield and regular participant of the various summer camps. He studied Engineering at King's College, Cambridge.

Letter 35 – 5 May 1914 (Summary)

In this letter dated 5 May 1914 Békássy quotes a long poem in French beginning with the line 'Voici le cavalier sans cheval' [Here is the Cavalier without a horse]. He also mentions that Peter Grant-Watson will be residing in Rupert Brooke's lodgings at the Vicarage, Grantchester, while the latter is in America. The letter ends with Békássy arranging to meet Noel at Victoria Station a few days later.

Letter 36 – 18 May 1914

In this letter, Békássy tells Noel that he has sent her his poem 'Adriatica'. The dedication to the poem, though not naming Noel, is clearly meant for her.

"You know the world of skies and hills and trees;
And, like a surge of waters, I send these
Lines to invade you: they are meant
A gift - a pleasure - an encouragement.
Take, if you will, whatever is the best;
Remember me; let others have the rest."

[Cambridge]

Sunday evening, 18 May 1914

Dear Noel,

I suppose you are now on the Broads somewhere; I wonder - it may even be Hickling, and Horsey Mere; or Brydon Water[1]; where two years ago, I sailed with Luce and Maynard etc. But I've forgotten most of the names, though I remember the evenings, the trees, and the look of the water, and one very red poppy-field (a field with very many poppies) on the Arcadian hillside. But that is connected with the poppies near Limpsfield, and the sailing's[2] connected with Luce, and a poem of his about Monkeys, who

'Locomoted on their tails
And called themselves the super-Mon
Wise fools and melancholy fun
They know the secret of their birth
For while the earth goes round the sun,
The sun must needs go round the earth!'

---

[1]   Place names on the Norfolk Broads.
[2]   sailing trip Békássy made with with John Maynard Keynes and Gordon Luce in 1913.

And all of it is connected to Adriatica[3] - I was writing it then- and a poem about a Swan, by Wordsworth (the Ode on Dion) and that is connected with the superb Leda (painting) by Michael Angelo, in the British Museum: and so with the Chinese Pictures Hugh [Popham] took me to see: and so it all goes round. Excuse the reminiscing, but you see how pleasant it is, just to think without restriction, if one dwells on each object. No doubt it shows a 'dreamy and vague and (vagabond) intellect', which Leonardo despised, but then...

I have just (it is 11.30 pm) come back from the Upper River, where two of us were canoeing. It is starry and mild; before that, I met an attractive, clever and probably unscrupulous lady of 40 (or less) with whom I had a conversation for a short while. Before that, I gave tea to Peter and a young lady of his acquaintance[4], and we were all in very high spirits. I played a game of chess before that, which was played by Capablanca[5] in a Tournament - but you can't know how exciting that is. I gave lunch to Shove and Lucas and another man, and they talked about Pope Sylvester II[6], and History and Ulster[7] and in the morning I did nothing. This is to break the monotony of a week's work.

However, when I have gone to bed I have never yet gone on thinking about work, but always about other things and people. By the way, it goes without saying that last week-end , with you, was - well! etc.: although - etc. (I've said it every time after I've been down to Limpsfield?)

---

[3]   A copy of which he also sent to Peter Grant-Watson, Justin Brooke and Gordon Luce for their comments.

[4]   Miss de Freyne, Peter Grant Watson's friend who according to Raisley Moorsom was 'not a lady' as she had said 'damn' when dropping her teaspoon. cf. Falkiner, *The Imago*, p. 222.

[5]   José Raul Capablanca (1888-1942) Cuban chess player, World Champion (1921-1927).

[6]   Sylvester II, Pope (999-1003).

[7]   Reference to the Home Rule Crisis.

My great hope now is that you will like Adriatica when you read it, and like everything in it about WATER, and like even the people - at least Anthony.[8] But, mon Dieu! What can I do? You will probably think it bad in places and good in others, and will not really care, and won't be able to think about the whole affair almost as if it had really happened and you remembered in some way (without having been there). - With all the self-consciousness of the present time, how could I write a thing that should carry conviction? Or how, do just what I intended?

I am dazed and tired and hate the society of my best friends. The last solid ground is disappearing from under my feet. I shall drop into space and I feel I shall never recover from that, but come out in some strange Antipodes.[9]

I must go to bed, I have been almost asleep, and thinking all sorts of imaginations.

What can I do, not to get quite dejected.

F. Békássy

---

[8]   Anthony, a character representing Békássy himself, who appears in Chapter 4 and 5 of 'Adriatica'.

[9]   The last outpost of the world in Greek mythology.

Letter 37 – 19 May 1914

[Cambridge]

Tuesday, 19 May 1914

Dear Noel,

Peter has been crushing about Adriatica: which does him little credit, I think for I refuse to believe all he says. It was like Rupert on Lyttonism.[1] However, I rather hope I shall not write anymore in English - the words sound empty to me, and my soul is filled with dust if I write. I am glad you liked it though.

Yes I do feel our generation is difficult, and almost agree with Lucas who says there is no activity fit for a decent person now, and hardly any society (20 people, not 200) - Of course old people have an answer as you said 'Coffee is just as good' (All Germans drink a huge glass of Coffee in their beds every morning!)

I am sometimes dazed, but then if I think of it, I have so many hopes about things that are beginning to happen - the undreamt of heights! So that it matters less that half the world is awry (an unprecedented thing) - It's 'only' a matter of continually and in everything choosing and selecting for oneself. I don't really belong to those who are unequal to doing this, or do something more difficult - although I almost do: and, when plunged into things will almost, but will never really belong to the 'City of Dreadful Night'[2] people. I only wish for many and definite Possibilities to believe in; I want to find my own Natural Assumptions, the things on which I act. It would be easy if I were something

---

[1] Peter Grant-Watson like Frances Cornford must have criticised the innuendos about homosexual relationships in 'Adriatica'. That is why Békássy compares him to Rupert on Lytton Strachey. Rupert hated Lytton for his open homosexuality, referring to him in a letter to Noel as 'Judas Iscariot'. *Song of Love*, p. 255.

[2] A long poem by Scottish poet James (B.V.) Thomson, who suffered from depression. The poem is about a London in which a poet has lost his faith and found nothing but emptiness to replace it.

definite like a Poet, a Journalist, a Pope of Rome - but I suppose I'm not. I am an Emanation of the Mental State called old Hungarian Gentry; gifted with the historical sight I float through the valleys of semi-detached imagination, where (as someone said) the lights of Piccadilly are seen for a moment by the soul on its ~~way~~ passage through the mists to Hades. Caught in the meshes and obstructions of Simple Fact, I slip from them as best I can, plunging and gliding and tortuously winding past the convolutions of the Brain (a Labyrinth); the law I perceive is the law of the serpent, and the flavour of mediation is on my tongue. My world is a river which eddies with small jets and fibres of water; in which no knot is cut, and the general necessity proves a force potent to loose and draw out every twisted, flexible knot of a whirlpool - however, I suppose you are not at ease when I assume airs, and I had better begin to talk sensibly.

It is very difficult - when I am on the verge of panic about my work. But now that it is warm, I bathe - which makes a difference. I also go up the river with Peter, and for his sake even bathed at the Bathing Sheds with a crowd of inexpressibly vulgarly horrible Ordinary Undergraduates with brillianted [sic] hair; and I put on a THING round myself to bathe in, - when by going above Byron's Pool,[3] I might have been above and in meadows.

<u>After</u> my Tripos, I shall go to Jaques' - when I shall be quite weak and unassuming. Gwen's large picture is at the Cornfords, where I steal a look at it now and then, love it, and admire her for it.

I didn't mean Pauly's kind of Antipodes,[4] though perhaps I may get there too - he does live a suitable life. I wish I knew

---

[3]   Byron's Pool, a bathing place on the River Cam, near Rupert Brooke's home in Grantchester, (named after Lord Byron who was supposed to have bathed there).

[4]   Paul Montague, old Bedalian who had gone the previous year on an expedition to New Caledonia, not returning until April 1915, *Song of Love*, p. 263.

him better. I like him and he is in some way quite extraordinary and almost (I don't mean this to offend) freakish. (Of course.) I envy him his accomplishments.

I wrote the last letter only two days ago - but that's no matter, I suppose - I mean, unless this bores you, it needn't offend?

Yours
F. Békássy

I hardly know how to bear twelve more days[5] - every moment gets pulled out (like toffy) almost indefinitely. So, when I look back, anything that happened an hour or a day ago is in the dim distance of years. Time must be like that, in Hell.

---

[5]   Until his final exams.

Letter 38 – 4 June 1914

[Cambridge]

[4 June 1914]

Dear Noel,

I finished my Tripos today; my last impression is, seeing rows of faces with knit brows, and one man gnawing his nails, while I was trying to think how to go on after 'contentment in the full exercise of all human faculties, which is happiness' - Since then, I have crammed as much into my dull day as it would bear. I lunched and drunk Champagne; and under its effects forced a most amazing victory at Chess - winning an advantage by a successful opening forced exchange after exchange on Stokoe (with whom I play) till I couldn't help winning, just by having one piece left.

Meanwhile I smoke his big German pipe with the birch bowl and cherry-wood stem - a great favour - and he read me a letter from Luce about his vast escapade, - descriptions of scenery and glaciers 20,000 feet;

Home

Of every vital element, where art,
Careless of old economy, converts
Magnificence to beauty.
(as he wrote)[1]

I went for a ride in the evening, all by myself, along absurd ways and with no consideration for the hardness of the ground. At dinner at the Union, I chattered and talked

---

[1] Gordon Luce was writing to Frank Stokoe from Burma.

nonsense, and then heard Signor Marinetti.[2] He came in a spick and span Italian, respectable with his bow tie and bald forehead, and florid and twirling a trivial moustache, a worldly man whose like you could meet anywhere and never notice. BUT he had a devil, like the people in the New Testament. It got into him and made him vehement in expounding his damnable and consistent theory; and towards the end when he declaimed a poem: 'The Bridge', a scene from the Balkan war ('free-words and noises') it wrestled with him and made him shriek and throw his arms about, till onomatopoeic Pandemonium recalled the monstrous nightmare and crude physical emotions of a fight.

You laugh; but it was ~~Art~~ art; only it had the devil in it. Of course it wasn't really art - not Olympian Art, but it had all the semblance without the soul, like Americans whom (they say) the Devil has created and made mechanically like men, but he couldn't give them a soul.

Later I talked with Dickinson; he said all women were too personal to <u>think</u> (thinking meaning a chain of abstract logic) and when they did, it was an inferior imitation of <u>US</u>; and that they all had vast experience and would never spend their time on Aberrations of the mind. It's a bad look out isn't it, and you might feel slighted!

You can't imagine the complications of my circumstances. I am steeped in other people's adventures, and all these 3 days while I did 12 hour's work a day, I was reading about South America; also Benvenuto Cellini;[3] and the Memoirs of Jean

<hr />

[2]   Philippo Tommaso Marinetti (1876-1944) Italian poet and adventurer read his
      poems at the Cambridge Union Society. Author of the Futurist Manifesto,1909
      in which he advocates the glorification of war. He became a war correspondent
      covering the Abyssinian and Balkan Wars and was an early supporter of the Fascist
      movement. Moorsom in his diaries refers to this poetry evening, noting that
      Marinetti read in 'staccato' French.
[3]   Benvenuto Cellini (1500-1571) Italian Goldsmith, sculptor and writer.

Cavalier, Protestant rebel general, Savoyard Condottiere, and finally Governor of Jersey.[4]

Just before I began my exams I went off to the Jacques! I went a cycle-ride with Jacques and at first he was mad, but later we drank strong ale and he came off the perch, and was very nice. I slept at their place; larks - stars - nightingales. Gwen is painting a Pietà which is of course <u>great</u>. She is very admirable. If the weather is good I shall spend all my time on the River. Peter Watson is gone now[5] and I of course am worse off without him, but can hardly miss anyone now—I am so detached. When shall I see you? You impressed me so when we rode here, by looking as though you were in the middle of a whirlwind, horse and all.

Yours
F. Békássy

---

[4] Jean Cavalier (1681-1740) leader of the French Huguenot insurgents known as the Camisards from 1702-1704. After the failed attempt to secure religious freedom from the French government, he fled to Switzerland and settled in a Huguenot colony in Ireland. His *Memoirs of the Wars of the Cevennes* was published in Dublin,1726.

[5] A few weeks later, Békássy joined Peter Grant-Watson in Switzerland, where on 28 June they heard of the assassination of Franz Ferdinand.

Letter 39 – 19 June 1914

38 Brunswick Square[1]
W.C. Telephone,7267
CITY

Friday, 19 June 1914

Dear Noel,

Isn't it possible to see you - not in a crowd or party, but by yourself (more or less) say tomorrow, at your place, or any time at and any occasion ~~place~~ you like. After all, one ought to have a good deal to talk about, and I am no use in company. Don't trouble to answer, though, if you don't approve, or if you are too busy about drugs and pancreas etc.

F. Békássy

---

[1] Home of Adrian Stephens and Virginia and Leonard Woolf, shared with other members of the Bloomsbury Group. Keynes also had rooms in the same building and Békássy used it occasionally when he was in London.

Letter 40 – 22 June 1914

Cambridge

Monday night, 22 June 1914[1]

Dear Noel,

I must write, to say something of what I thought of yesterday, that is to say that <u>it</u>, like some other occasions: one day last year (this time and at Marlboro Rd, an afternoon and evening, one day, planting flowers at Limpsfield; the first time I went to Limpsfield and a walk in the rain; and the time (afternoon) in the Bedales Library, when you wrote me down that poem of Stevenson's - but I see the sentence has got too long. There were many occasions.

What I want to say is that I remember them, and that I shall remember yesterday (and the others) more often than anything that has happened to me in England. You never believed my saying I liked them, you thought they must hurt, and of course they do, ~~and~~ but it doesn't matter.

Whenever I in the least degree show that I care for you, you seem troubled and upset or annoyed, or - whatever it is. I don't know what it is, and thought all sorts of things at times, that it was the way things happened, or would not last, or that I cut a too ridiculous figure and what you write and say we had better not meet any more (last September) - but that I may go on writing(!) I don't take it seriously because you don't mean that; but yesterday I felt it was all much more final (as final as though I had really said a great deal more than I did.) What I ~~felt yesterday~~ feel is not any sort of infatuation nor is it imaginary nor a bad growth on our good relations to each other. It has gone on all the time (except when two years

---

ago I was for a week at Limpsfield) and without anything ever happening, so that my desires have quite encased themselves and at times I simply have no active desires when I think of you and see you; but that's not the point. But ALL the time (<u>always</u>) I KNOW that we do in the natural course of the universe BELONG together and to each other. Whenever I see that you clearly don't think so, I am at my wit's end, it seems to me it is so obvious etc.- Forgive this incredible arrogance, Please! - I don't want to hedge. That is the way I love you, if <u>you</u> want to call it that: <u>I</u> do.

I suppose you had much rather that I didn't call it or feel it that. God knows what other use I can be, and all this talk you make me go on with (and it's so easy to set me on to an idea and make me go on: - because I like it.) But at any rate though of course I have acquiesced and not really ever gone on saying what I sometimes began, I want to say that all this (just because it was like this) has been the most important thing for me.

You see it is still the most important. I don't imagine my feelings will always be the same and I may fall in love or marry twenty times, but that's not the point: and I wish I wasn't going to, because it <u>can't</u> have the same roots and rightness which I <u>know</u> this has. I don't think it's a question <u>only</u> of feeling but of nature.

I am writing now only BECAUSE I shall see you again several times and this isn't a 'last word' but I want to see if we can meet again after it. Please don't mind it and get alarmed, there wouldn't be any sense in doing that, now there is hardly any more time left. All this that I have said seems to me not anything that alters our relations because it was there before.

Of course I am not posing as if going away for more than a year or two, but that seems to me a long time. I don't want to write during it, - if I can help it, but perhaps I shan't be able to.

When I went to Bryn's[2] it was all very suitable and fitted in with the whole day. I wonder if Bryn knew how very good she was just in going on and making me play cards and looking after me and letting me sleep there and saying I fitted in quite well. And saying a kind word now and then and not letting me be very serious.

This letter is serious, but that can't be helped. I'm not, at least not always, so perhaps seeing me again won't be too beastly for you.

I suppose I had better send this. The tone is dreadful, but you know it isn't quite what it seems, and as for the rest it is TRUE. I hope all of it is true, and so you had better know (though you knew all of it already). As I have only said what always existed, it will perhaps make NO difference for the next fortnight. Please don't think I don't realise it is and has been rather beastly (and difficult?) for you, but if one takes each occasion separately - for instance, yesterday - don't you think we had quite a decent, pleasant, good day? I do. It's that I don't want to spoil[it] with too much seriousness.

Yours, body and soul and altogether, only it's not much use is it?

F. Békássy

---

2   Bryn's marital home was also in Bloomsbury.

Letter 41 – July 1914

As there is no envelope to this letter it is difficult to date. We know that Békássy was in Switzerland on holiday, where he heard the news of the assassination of Franz Ferdinand on 28 June (see Introduction). He must then have returned to England as there is a letter to Constance Garnett written in England dated 7 July. His next letter to her was written from Hungary on 29 July but it reached her only after the war. (Both the Garnett letters are included in this volume) Noel inserted her own comments in the letter and underlined certain lines, for which we have used italics. She did not, however, send the letter back to Békássy.

Kis Sennye Rum Vas vm.

July 1914

Dear Noel,

I said I wouldn't write, but that was silly - at least I think so, but please say what you think, because perhaps it would be a relief to you if I didn't write: and it wouldn't make <u>very</u> much difference to me now. *No, go on writing*

Altogether - I wish I knew what you thought. Is it too much to ask? You can't 'hurt my feelings' whatever you say: I'm not English!

You see, I wonder did you <u>sometimes</u> think it would be much more convenient <u>if we had nothing to do with each other?</u> *No* or did you think <u>it was really pleasant to think I was in love with you,</u> *No* though of course <u>it was wretched</u> it was because it made me unhappy and so it would from a <u>humanitarian point of view be better if I wasn't?</u> *no, not from a humanist point of view* <u>or that it was all right as long as you didn't get entangled?</u> Once at Bedales you said to - was it Dorothy?[1] - who wanted to leave us alone and thought that tactful,: 'we' (you and myself) are '<u>grown up</u> now' intimating that she should stay. Do you

---

[1]   Dorothy Winser.

still think that, i.e. that <u>skull-bones and lymphatic glands are more important?</u> *No.* <u>And that camps are the acme of human relationships?</u> *between and* [sic] *most people: –Yes.* There are such a lot of people who admire/love/adore (etc.) you, <u>do you wish there were none</u>, *No* or that they all <u>behaved as though they didn't</u>, *in relation to my feelings* but still went on doing it? Or was it just a <u>personal question</u> so that I am to be jealous of the others? *yes, because your behaviour was particular.*

I expect there was something you wanted from me and I went and spoilt it all by wanting something quite different: I mean the way you said (in that letter about not wanting to see me again) that our conversations had been the best thing in our acquaintance and we could do <u>that</u> by writing letters.

But I see I'm missing the point, there is probably something I haven't asked, which is at the bottom of the whole thing. Would you like to answer, and say what you think, and write as if you were compiling a psychological treatise?

When I went away from England I found that there were quite several people more sorry than I. I wasn't hurt by it, it was like an operation under an anaesthetic, and now here I sit convalescent, having nobody in the world except a mother and a brother and sister or two - but no one else.

You will be at the O.B. meeting now, or soon: but I feel it would be a strain to be there, though I'd enjoy it. Later, I suppose there are camps and things - yes of course I didn't mean that a camp isn't a very enjoyable thing, it's the greatest fun in the world.

It is just possible that one day I'll have a house and a place. I shall then invite all the people I know in England, and make them live a month among vineyards and forests and in Hungary. You will <u>have</u> to come then, and all the others.

I'm afraid I never said goodbye to anyone except you and Bryn, and don't even remember when I saw Daphne for the last time; can one make up for this by wishing it had turned out differently?

Do write. Please! and tell me what you used to think of me (*!!*)

Yours
F. Békássy

Letter 42 – September 1914

Békássy sent the following letter to William Burdet, a friend and old Bedalian living in Switzerland, who with some delay and a covering note (the envelope is postmarked 16 November) forwarded it to Noel. It had been opened but allowed through by the British Censor. Noel mentions receiving it, in a letter to Rupert Brooke dated 7 January 1915. (Song of Love, p.277)

I am writing Noel from my garrison,[1] expecting in a few weeks or less to be called to the front. I am going easily with a good conscience but I must write to you and say everything. I didn't know how to say it when I saw you, I meant to say, forgive me for having been too persistent. I know you don't want me to be anything more to you than a boy you knew at school and saw occasionally afterwards and liked or did not and who bored you or did not, just like all the others. Well now you have what you wished and that is all I am to you and I ought not and shall not try to claim anything more. I was always trying to but how could I help it and how can I help now being full of regrets because I saw all the time the kind of thing that I imagined might happen about us two and how surely we ought to have more than we had to do with each other, and you did not see it and there never was anything. You must let me say it like this, you I suppose would say I was wrong, but I am only excusing my keeping on so; (because it must have been annoying and it <u>did </u>make you want not to see me anymore). And although I could cry because of all that hasn't happened and might have, I am not wretched and it has anyhow been very good. I think you don't know how good it has been for me and perhaps you think happiness matters more - but I own I was unhappy and say that happiness does not matter <u>at all</u> compared to goodness.

---

[1]   This letter is written from the garrison in Pápa, Western Hungary, where Békássy received his military training.

I can't tell you how all the feelings and impulses and ideas which you will always stand for (in that private world of mine which belongs to nobody else) but the best part of myself was made up of them for these three or four years. All the same, it would be ridiculous of me to make much ado about it all, (please forgive this, it is not spite) as though I come and go and find something for myself, and this which didn't happen (one can't do it by himself, a lover is somebody who is loved and well 'there was' as you say 'nothing'. I mean to you it was nothing) is just one more unrealised idea. So I shall go to the war and not think about you and be on the lookout for something else. I hope when we meet again we shall get on all right, and if we don't meet - well, it won't be my fault and one can't help taking risks. But if <u>you</u> ever have any regrets, don't take them seriously - they're not dangerous.

B.

(Yours - if you could have wanted to keep him but it may be as well otherwise).

I couldn't anyhow write news and it isn't allowed. I am very overworked but well off. Don't believe everything in the papers. I think these times are changing me a great deal; all you, I suppose are safe and well. Tell the others anything about me, but if Luce comes to England, give him my love.

Letter 43 – May 1915

Noel received the following letter with news of Békássy's death while on holiday in Switzerland, postmarked 9 July 1915. It was sent to her with the covering letter by his sister Éva, who gives the wrong date for Békássy's death, which was in fact the 25ᵗʰ June. In her previous letter Noel must have given her address in Switzerland.

Budapest

May 1915

Dear Noel,

Very many thanks for your letter, really you don't know how good it was to get. I am going to the front in five days' time, and am already feeling quite detached from everything so that nothing interests me very much and the only vivid remembrances are: people. A week ago I still thought a lot about how sad it was that 38 Br. Square had broken up and that everything among you is changing, though I had felt it would never change, and how sad it is that I suppose things will never be quite the same again, and that the last four years were so splendid. But now I can only think of you (and the others) and you know, Noel, it is all the times that we two met, that I most like to remember - from the time at Bedales when you wrote 'Under a wide and starry sky' down for me, to the last time we met, at Bedales; and not excepting any single meeting either! I wonder whether everything that happened before the war will seem quite far-away afterwards?

It's a year almost, since I've left - I was in Switzerland with Peter last June. The time has gone so fast, I feel as though someone had robbed a year out of my life - because, though it has been very instructive of course (I got to know Budapest and Jews and business and women and the 'social order') - it

<u>hasn't</u> been <u>my</u> life. I think it will be, when I go. I'm going gladly, I know it's very worth taking the risk, and I am sure to get something good out of the war unless I die in it. It's part of 'the good life' just now, that <u>I</u> should go: and the sooner one gives up the idea that the <u>world</u> can be made better than it is, the better. I daresay one can make it happier, but then happiness isn't the main point, is it?

Since the war began, I have written poems again, I think they are good but it's no use writing for <u>this</u> public! — Everything is beautiful now, there are some evenings in which all the lovely things are heaped together, flower-smells, clouds, water, chestnut-trees, and young corn. There are very beautiful sunsets, and all this makes it somehow easier to go. I've come to think everything is more important about lives than when they end; because, when I die, someone else is born instead, so it really doesn't matter, (but this is so impersonal that one can only think it when there's no occasion.) I wanted to write much more about May and the country. Do you know I think there's a difference between poets (who write poetry) and other people, that poets take hold of the feelings they have and won't let go; and other people let feelings have their natural effects and so don't write poems. I must be changing a good deal now - at any rate outwardly, and that's what seems to matter in one's relations to people. I can't believe I've altogether left all of you though it seems definite enough - and perhaps the war won't stop till everyone is too tired to be good for anything. People are getting so used to the war. By the time I go, there'll be roses, and I shall go with a crest of three red ones on my horse's head because (but people won't know the reason) there are three over the shield in our coat of arms.

This isn't at all the letter I meant to write, but I can't help it. I long to see you, and all of you again. I often think of you.

And we shall meet, Noel, shan't we, some day?

Good-bye,

Yours

F. Békássy[1]

[*covering note sent with the above letter*]

Kis Sennye Rum Vas vm.

4 July 1915

Dear Noel,

It is just the sad conclusion I can add to this letter: its writer lives no more. It is only a few weeks ago he left for the front, full of life and vigour and ever since then he was always in the worst place and took part in the most terrible battles.

On May the 25th his regiment (the 7th Royal Hungarian honor'd hussars) had a terrible battle in which he (and many others) lost his Life.

You must excuse this short scrappy note but it is all I am able to write

Yours

Eva Békássy

---

[1]   It is the only time Békássy signs his letter with the words 'goodbye', a presentiment.

Noel with baby son Ben, in 1924

John Maynard Keynes, about 1911

LETTERS TO
JOHN MAYNARD KEYNES

John Maynard Keynes (1883-1946)

John Maynard Keynes, one of the most influential economists of the twentieth century, was born into a Cambridge academic family. He was educated at Eton and King's College, Cambridge, where he became Fellow in 1908. A year later he accepted a lectureship in economics. His first major publication was *Indian Currency and Finance* (1913) and while formally not a member of the civil service, he acted as Economic Adviser to the British Government in 1914. As financial representative for the Treasury he took part in the Versailles peace conference, but he did not agree with the harsh conditions imposed by the Allies, calling them, according to his biographer Richard Davenport-Hines, "outrageous and impossible" (*Universal Man*, 2015). Having resigned from the Treasury he went back to teaching at Cambridge, becoming Bursar of King's College in 1924. It was here that he wrote his main and most influential work, *The General Theory of Employment, Interest and Money*. In 1942 he became a peer, receiving the title Baron Keynes of Tilton. After the Second World War

Keynes was instrumental in setting up the World Bank and the International Monetary Fund.

Keynes's early sexual relationships were exclusively with men. Some of these were members of 'The Apostles', the exclusive Cambridge debating society. One of his long relationships was with the artist Duncan Grant whom Davenport-Hines describes as "the most important man in Keynes's life". When Békássy arrived in Cambridge in the autumn of 1911 Keynes was immediately struck by this rich, outstandingly intelligent, Hungarian poet and took him under his wing.

How much this had to do with physical attraction is debatable; nevertheless Keynes visited the Békássy family in Hungary in September 1912. He was also instrumental in preserving his young friend's memory, financing the posthumous volume of his poetry published by Hogarth Press.

After World War I, Keynes fell in love with Russian ballerina Lydia Lopokova whom he married in 1925.

Letter 1 to Keynes – 18 March 1912

[Postcard]
18 March 1912

Dear Maynard,

Go to the Union and find out the address of what I think is called the 'Historical Review'.[1] Then write it down on a P.C. and send to Mrs. N. Jarintzoff,[2] The White House, Petersfield , Hants.

Yrs. br.[brotherly?]
Feri

P.S. Mrs. J. has written a grand article which she wants to send to the Review. Another person is writing an article on the same thing in another monthly. The affair is therefore urgent.

I suppose it's too much to ask you to write to me in Hungary about Rupert[3], but I am dying to know.

---

[1] Correct title *The English Historical Review*, founded in 1886.
[2] Nadine Jarintzoff - see Noel Letter 7, footnote 5.
[3] Referring to Rupert Brooke who was recuperating from a nervous breakdown in the South of France and Germany.

Letter 2 to Keynes – April 1912

[Kis-Zsennye, Hungary]
[April] 1912

Dear Maynard,

To get over business first: you might have remembered. We Are Seven. Six of us still left,[1] that is one more [sic] than in Wordsworth. Neither the masculine nor the feminine element is preponderant. I mean, neither boys nor girls are in a majority. 3:3.

To proceed: I am quite alone; outside the grass is smothered in flowers, it is raining and there is a strong north wind. The rooms have been empty since Xmas and their condition is appalling. I have nothing to do but to admire everything in turn, and count the keys over and over again. The tops of fir trees are scratching at the wall below my window. The rest of the family are straggling home and will arrive during tomorrow and the day after.

The most sensational news is that the King[2] has been sensible and that the heir presumptive[3] was behind this crisis, carrying on a flirtation with the clericals. The old government is returning[4], and my father is not going to resign, etc.[5]

But for the next 40 years - after this government *does* fall - the whole country will be smothered in clericalism. All my generation are intensely clerical. I shall be here for the worst

---

[1] One of the Békássy siblings died in infancy.

[2] Franz Joseph I, Emperor of the Austro-Hungarian Monarchy, King of Hungary (1830-1916).

[3] Archduke Franz Ferdinand (1863-1914) later assassinated on 28th June 1914 at Sarajevo.

[4] The Nationalist and Clerical opposition had overthrown the Liberal Government led by Prime Minister Khuen-Héderváry, but the King had the power to reinstate them under a new Prime Minister, László Lukács, formerly a member of the cabinet.

[5] Békássy's father István Békássy was *főispán*, the equivalent of Lord Lieutenant of Vas County, a position appointed by the government.

of it. At the Budapest University one has to be a Clerical or a Philo-Jew, and arrange one's opinions on matters of learning accordingly. Those of the landed gentry (the only class that counts in politics) who aren't clerical are retiring.

Before I came here to repent and renounce my sins I debauched in town, coming in for the very end of the season. But it was dull.

At any rate I have become quite Hungarian by now; nothing is more absurd than the idea of my thinking in English. There are three perpendicular lines between my eyebrows; my lips have an expressive curl; and the peasant-women kiss my hand, as though I were a bishop. Perhaps I might add, a *young* bishop.

I don't ever want to see Cambridge again. Nothing need ever happen, really, I might just as well say here, go out to shoot duck in the evenings, keep bees, and read the classics, and be glad I've got some brains.

I am in perpetual excitement about the fate of Gerald Shove's[6] five franc pieces. I think gambling is rather a strain on one's nerves, I almost wish you hadn't drawn *me* into it. Besides, I have never been at Monte Carlo, and you left me to find out for myself how the game works. - Anyhow, I suppose Gerald has got you to lose all your money by now, and the Bank has sent you home with a 2nd class ticket. That is what happens to heroes in our novels. If the writer is a preacher at the beginning of the book, a critic at the end and is a decadent all the way through.

Other things I've done - besides riding with my sister and others - and that have happened are too unintelligible for me to tell you about them.

I don't want to go to bed yet because a cart (furniture) that ought to have come (everything's upside down) has not arrived

---

6   Gerald Shove, see Main Characters. Shove and Keynes were on holiday in the South of France and visited Monte Carlo.

yet. If it were not raining so abominably etc., I would go out to meet it. I suppose Rupert will get his fellowship next year anyhow.[7] I don't want to think about people or English and Cambridge things. I am full of things I dare not write because they sound ridiculous and I go mad when I think about them. What on earth am I to do *all* next term?

(You see I had to end up somehow like this, it would have been too undramatic otherwise. This, at any rate, is mildly melodramatic. I like to have some proof that I really have been feeling feelings I have imagined for myself. This is getting complicated).

Yours sr.
Feri

---

7   Rupert Brooke did receive his Fellowship in March 1913.

Letter 3 to Keynes – July 1912

Kis Sennye, Rum, Hungary

July 1912

[Ferenc Békássy to John Maynard Keynes]
[…]

These sort of things[1] - I mean attempts at rain - have been going on for some time. Meanwhile there is nothing to write. Here, it's impossible to get aeroplanes, though one might fly between 6 and 7a.m. How do you manage?

We play tennis, but we don't … I mean, there isn't a lawn. I was also at a dinner etc. in the town a while ago, but - que Diable allai-je faire dans cette galère?[2]

I didn't know Lucy[3] would be there.[4] Has he got to the last lines of his sonnet yet? […]

I hope you are not cast onto each other's sympathy and almost on the point of breaking down; Ka isn't there and I hope you wouldn't trust yourself to an Olivier's tender mercies.

But perhaps the fervid influences of my ruling planet (Mars; that's the reason for my ruthless intellect etc.) will for a time drive out all watery and murky humours from your anatomy. At any rate, until you come.

Yours,
Feri

---

[1] Referring to the omitted first half of this letter about the weather, in the form of a comic verse.

[2] Paraphrase from *Les Fourbieries de Scapin*. a play by Molière (1622-1673) 'Que diable allait-il faire dans cette galère?'. (What the Devil shall he do in this 'hell-hole'?).

[3] Gordon Luce, see Main Characters.

[4] Keynes had booked the Crown Hotel at Everleigh at the end of July 1912 for a reading party. Bryn, Daphne and Noel Olivier were present. Ka Cox, Rupert Brooke's then girlfriend, did not attend. Nigel Jones, p. 268.

[P.S]

Does this piece of etymology interest you? - In the XII century there sprang up a sect - the Cathari - whose 'haeretica pravitas'[5] was, in fine, a new Manichaeism,[6] imported into Western Europe by the Bogumils, the holy men of Bulgaria. Hence the popular name of these Cathari was (French) *bougres*, and *bougrerie* meant heresy. But that made their doctrine more extreme; the soul was imprisoned by the Devil in the flesh: <u>marriage</u> therefore a betrayal of God. These cathari grew greatly in numbers; the converts were men young, and 'ardent with the new tendencies of the time'.*

The rest of my tribe are coming in a week; meanwhile I am still a snowdrop (because my sister III[7] kindly explained today, 'you're all right when there's nothing else, but when <u>they</u> come...)

*How people accuse innocent Bulgaria![8]

F.B.

---

[5]   Heretical deviation (Latin).

[6]   A dualistic religious system with a doctrine of the conflict between good and evil.

[7]   Békássy's youngest sister Klára.

[8]   [FB note].

Letter 4 to Keynes – July 1912

Kis-Zsennye, Hungary

July 1912[1]

> Trunk-things floating, sisters gloating - dreary prospect,
>   you'll agree -
> Still unpacking, yawning, slacking: very hot and half
>   past three.
> This to ease me - if it please me - so again you hear
>   from me.
>
> 'Hardly settled down to Sennye; 'nothing write of that
>   self, here,
> So you picture (- it's a stricture -) that at any rate is clear.
> Just an hour from the journey; now the news! What?
>   None to hear?
>
> 'Oh, the Bishop! How they've fished up sacramental
>   ornaments
> -Operation-inflammation-here official knowledge ends;'
> 'X and miss S and their blisses' - country scandal twists
>   and bends.
>
> And 'the corn is rain down-beaten; worms have crunched
>   and chafers eaten,
> Gnawed the very heart of roses; nothing on the plumb-
>   tree rows is.'
> 'Then the balls at Mrs H's; dancers rubbing knees
>   and noses.'

---

[1]   Letter in verse parodying Robert Browning's 'A Toccata of Galuppi's', written upon Békássy's return to Hungary, recollecting parties and their mutual activities back in England.

So forth. Journey! Such a journey! Long and sooty,
     dull enough;
Had a neighbour (purple, pouchy, leery-eyed, in a manner
     bluff)
Told me, how his wife's aunt's cousin's daughter had the
     whooping-cough!

...Was a country such a country, was a lady such a ...
Where we clomb the Calycanthus,[2] leaping as with
     locusts' wings,
And where nightly James talked rightly, in the shrubs, of
     Love and things?

(For we slept beneath the heavens when the heavens were
     good enow).
Where we'd Parsons, murders, arson - (well we acted, all
     allow)
Yonke Danky Do-s and donkeys, stuff and nonsense. -
     Well, and now? -

To the circles where no Turtles swiftly scurry, ah,
     where James
Feels at home, once being up to peoples' tricks and
     little games
Greeting (but I hope you will not let him call me
     beastly name).

What with James[3] and Jews and Browning,
Soon I left them, sadly frowning

---

[2]   Deciduous shrub.
[3]   James Strachey, see Main Characters.

As Lord Howard's[4] consort drove me down to Oxted,[5]
    rain-pour-down-ing

Just as Rupert[6] - but 'tis stupid,[7] - I'm too tired to tell
    the rest.
So remain in *Son* and *Father* and the Holy Spirit blest,
(Nerves not weak'ning) beauty-seeking brainy brothers
    of the West!

Feri

---

[4] Lord Howard, Earl of Effingham, neighbour of the Oliviers.
[5] Nearest railway station to Limpsfield, the Olivier's home.
[6] Rupert Brooke.
[7] [FB note] at bottom of letter 'with apologies to Rupert'.

Letter 5 to Keynes – 5 August 1912

Kis-Zsennye, Rum, Vas vm.

5 August 1912

Dear Maynard,

The 16th will do admirably. After the 18th there will only be four of 'us children' here, my eldest sister, my 'twin' brother and my youngest sister, besides myself. (I hope you won't find it too few, nor too many, not too much!)

At Vienna you book from the Sudbahnhof to RÁBAMOLNÁRI (rah'bo-mol-naahry) but the train is just 'nach Ungarn.'[1] Probably you'll come starting at... a.m. arriving about... p.m. You can get a dinner (if you think you'll be able to eat it) brought into the carriage at Sopron, if you tell the guard soon after Wiener-Neustadt. At about... you get to Szombathely (Steinamanger): there look out of the window for five minutes, I might be there. You might bring a black coat and something to ride in, other things don't matter. (What you will ride on, I don't quite know yet. Don't expect something too grand).

Unless you can convince me of the contrary, I shall go on believing you're arriving on the 16th by that train: though it's almost incredible, Cambridge and all you being so very far. The only other news I had's from Noel, who is in Switzerland, described your Inn [Crown Hotel, Everleigh] in glowing language, and told of Bryn's engagement. What Popham? Hugh![2] (Expression of red Indians used for feelings {see Karl May}[3] which we in ordinary language have no way of

---

[1]   'To Hungary': in the next couple of lines there are spaces in the original where Békássy forgets to fill in the times of the trains.

[2]   Noel's sister Brynhild became engaged to Hugh Popham.

[3]   Karl May (1842-1912) German author, his most popular works read throughout Europe were his stories about Red Indians in the American Old West.

rendering {see St. Thomas Aquinas}[4] and the others). It seems very silly, but then perhaps it isn't.

I wonder how you'll like it here, I think not much. Are you really intending to work steadily until your brain gives way?[5]

It seems I am going to the Tyrol with Tonika (elder sister) the day after tomorrow, but it's not quite settled yet. I don't know what to think of it; as a matter of fact it's like when I wake up in the early morning, want to go riding but would rather lie in bed and think or get up and do nothing: but am miserable for the rest of the day if I haven't ridden. The second crop of hay has been carted in just lately and one can ride all over the meadows.

Have you ever read Nietzsche[6] or doesn't Cambridge philosophy allow it? I wish you read *Beyond Good and Evil*, I like him so much: he seems the only person who really has launched out and struggled through in all the masses of thought that always seem to lead nowhere (beginning with things like *truth*, and so forth) so that whatever he says does come genuinely, and he never says things he believes 'in order that he may stand,' without mentioning that as the reason of his belief; one can deal honestly with him. You know I read him ages ago, and it seems strange to me now how much of him I understood then - but it's no use talking.

I am reading the Hungarian Classics (who begin at the end of the 18th century: down to the middle of the 19th). That too is a change, because they are all bad - unreadable - and I need to read like a butterfly, going only for beauty. But they made it possible for us to master our language (though we still have to do it each for himself, and an immense amount of talent

---

[4] Thomas Aquinas (1225-1274), in *Summa Theologica.*

[5] Keynes was working on his first book *Indian Currency and Finance*, published the following year.

[6] Friedrich Nietzsche, see Introduction, footnote 7. *Beyond Good and Evil* was published in 1886.

{among poets} is wasted because of this; unlike your poets who find a language that expresses their things for them) - and I am reading even their quarrels with tremendous enthusiasm.[7]

I am slack to go on writing down things and don't feel inclined to talk. So -

Yours
Feri

---

[7]   This refers to the quarrel in Hungary during the early part of the nineteen century, between the Neologists, that is language reformers, with the conservative linguists and writers.

Letter 6 to Keynes – September 1912

Schluderbach[1]

September 1912

Dear Maynard,

I retract all I ever said about black coats of any sort; please don't take any notice, - how *can* you ask *me* about clothes! *What* an idea!

But I'm an authority on routes. The usual one we go by is Quenboro' (or Folkestone), Flushing, Hanover, Leipzig, Dresden, Teschen, Vienna; that's the most direct, and one gets in one end and out at the other, having only to trouble about not committing suicide through sheer boredom in between. You must leave by the night boat so as to get to Vienna in the morning and Molnari at 4 p.m. as I said.

Then one might go up the Rhine which is less ugly and doesn't take much longer; Vlissingen (Flushing) as before; same train as before, but a different carriage, to Cologne; Cologne, Frankfurt, Munchen (Munich!) where you would get in the evening, as to Dresden; Vienna next morning (by Lienz).

Of course, you may like to visit some town you are fond of, e.g. Berlin, or Moscow, St. Petersburg, or Irkutsk; they are all very fine places, worth going to. To get to the first you go the same old Vlissingen-Hanover way (different direct carriage) and I suppose it would only take three days; to get to Vienna by Moscow might take five, St. Petersburg seven: Irkutsk - it is not safe to venture on any definite assertion.

I hope we'll manage the doddering back; I don't see why not as I haven't got a return ticket either. We might go to Berlin then?[2]

---

[1] Resort in the South Tyrol, Austria, now Italy.
[2] It appears that they did not travel back to England together.

It's so cold my fingers are quite numb - but I forgot, you don't even know I've been here (Aust., Tirol) for a fortnight with my eldest sister, Tonika; am going back tomorrow though.

Of course they haven't forwarded the literary supplement, for which many thanks. Still reviews on Rupert! He must be getting quite pleased by now about the way people take his poems.[3]

I wrote James[4] a silly letter after I got yours, as a cultured grandson might write to an old gentleman who is a staunch supporter of liberalism and professes all the great ideals and ideas new 30 years ago. But he must be getting tired of that joke by now. I was immensely amused by Lucy's poem,[5] I wonder where he is now.

Hotels! And the people in them! If I stay here longer my poetry too will reflect the hopeless failure of the (lower middle) i.e. citizen classes - as has been said lately *in praise* of a new Hungarian poet!!

Write if you're not arriving on 16th.

Yours
Feri

---

[3]   Rupert Brooke's first volume of poetry, *Poems* was published in 1911 by Sidgwick and Jackson and was reviewed in the *Times Literary Supplement* on 29 August 2012. Listed in *Friends and Apostles*, p. 297.

[4]   This letter to James Strachey is included in the present volume.

[5]   Gordon Luce.

Letter 7 to Keynes – 6 January 1915

An unposted letter from Békássy to John Maynard Keynes. It was written in January 1915, but was not posted. It was found by Békássy's mother after his death. After the end of the war Békássy's brother János (John), mentioned in the letter as being a prisoner of war on the Isle of Man, made a visit to Hungary. He took the letter back to England with him and posted it to Keynes from London with a covering letter on 23ʳᵈ. December 1920. [1]

Budapest, Üllöi út 115/B.I.

6 January 1915

My dear Maynard,

Why didn't you *write* instead of just arranging that I should do so? I know just as little about all of you, and would like to know just as badly.

Perhaps you have heard how my brother is on the Isle of Man in a prisoners' camp (No.1129, Peel)[2] I wanted to write and ask you to help him but Mr. Badley[3] did everything that was possible. Éva - whom Justin remembers,[4] at least he ought - writes sometimes, she of course is having a grand time. As for me - I am neither dead, nor have I been mutilated, nor have I been to the front yet, though here people said all these things about me. When I came home in August, I thought I would certainly be going in 6 or 8 weeks - and it was almost true, and since then I often thought we would be going, but now, after having been in a wretched little town for some months,[5] I am back in Budapest, where I am staying till March. It is too

---

[1] ACKC Keynes PP 45/24/26.

[2] Town on the Isle of Man.

[3] John H. Badley, see Introduction, footnote 3. It was in fact the pottery manufacturer Josiah Wedgwood who enabled János Békássy's release from internment. His daughter Rosamund married János in 1920.

[4] Éva Békássy and Justin Brooke, see Main Characters.

[5] The garrison at Pápa, Western Hungary.

long - I would like it best if I were going now - but perhaps
March will be time enough.

I am enjoying this soldier's life - I have become a swagger
horseman(!) a crack shot(!) and anything else you like, the brain
capacity decreasing in proportion to the accumulating brawn.
Before I came up here, I met and made friends with many -
now officers, but usually of course ordinary citizens - who
have mostly gone to the war and some are dead and some have
come back wounded - I went to see one just now, a splendid
lieutenant who taught me all I know about military matters.
Life in Budapest is almost as gay as ever and much more full of
sense and spirit - but I am occupied from 7 a.m. to 7 p.m. and
see comparatively little of it. Many of my relations are gone to
the war, and it was rather a sad Christmas, but the New Year
brought Tonika's husband[6] back to her for two days.

I hardly know what to write. I am simply WAITING and
WANTING to DO something. I can't write about what I think
of the war,[7] and even if I could I would hate to, I want to *be
in it* and forget what I think.

I am already firmly rooted in Hungary, as of course I knew
I would be when I came home - when I come back to you it
will be for a visit only.

Write and tell me about *everybody*; I was ill a few weeks
ago, and thought of you all, all the time. Tell me what Lucy
is doing, one hardly knows whether his part of the world is
peaceful or not.[8] Tell me how the Society[9] continues - the
only undisturbed thing in these times. Lucas I know is splendid:
has he found anyone else?[10] And tell me please about Noel, if

---

6   Antonia's husband József Görgey.
7   Reference to the letters being censored.
8   Gordon Luce was by this time teaching in Rangoon, Burma.
9   The Apostles.
10 Frank Laurence (Peter) Lucas (see Main Characters) was elected to the Apostles
    in 1914.

there is anything to tell.

Of course, Budapest is full of hospitals, but it only makes people more full of spirit if they're occupied most of the day, and it's a morally good occupation, looking after the wounded.

I suppose the war touches you much less than us. - I am glad and at the same time am embittered when I think of things - but the good people always have the best of everything (it's easy for us) and I am only annoyed because the others always make a mess for themselves. -

I have been with my cousin [Flora] at her hospital and saw all the different nations - Bohemians who can't bear pain, but the loss of a limb causes them no mental suffering (a Hungarian would rather die than be a cripple), the patient Russians, and the various Ruthenians and Rumanians who are quite like animals, and a lot more - Poles who can amuse a whole room, and one who we thought was dying, began to sing Polish songs on Christmas eve. He had two voices and I thought one was a woman singing - but all Poles are gifted! There are persistent Germans and *krautig*[11] Austrians but of course the Hungarians (the peasants) seem almost an aristocracy of intelligence among them all.

I very much wonder how you take IT - some adventurous spirit whom you despise - perhaps (but I don't feel at all sure) Watson[12] will have gone to the war. Of course I am writing poems but that's not what I'd really like to be writing now - one can't write anything else though it's only poems one can spin out of nothing. (To create is to make something out of nothing, says the Catechism!) It's too late and I must of course get up early, and I am sleepy and can't write.

Write about everyone and everything. I suppose in England there is the same idiotic hatred of the inimical nations as here.

---

[11] *Kraut*, hence '*krautig*' offensive slang for German.
[12] Elliot Logwood (Peter) Grant -Watson, see Main Characters.

For myself and unless I die in it, I shall have got nothing but good out of this war. Love to everybody, a different kind to each - and choose which you like, for yourself.

Feri

LETTER TO
JOHN TRESSIDER SHEPPARD

John Tressider Sheppard (1881-1968)

Sheppard studied classics at King's College, Cambridge, becoming a Fellow there in 1908. He was the first non-Etonian to become Provost of the College in 1933, a post he held until 1954. He was knighted in 1950 for his work on Greek culture. His publications include *The Pattern of the Iliad* and *Greek Tragedy*.

He was Senior Tutor at King's, tutoring Rupert Brooke and as a member of the 'Apostles' and good friend of Keynes, also became close to Békássy.

Letter to Sheppard – 21 June 1912

Riversdale,
Goring, Oxford[1]

21 June 1912

Dear Sheppard,

There is a book who runs may <u>not</u> read[2] - I mean I can't get hold of it. By Robert Browning, on 'The Poet Subjective and Objective; Shelley The…' (I forget what). An Essay. Published I think about 1850.[3]

The University Library is not yet closed. If you get it out <u>now </u>and send it to me here, I don't mind paying a reasonable fine (6/-) provided I can keep it till September. Or are they absurd and have they got cumulative fines?

Perhaps the Union might have it, too. There is only 2/6 to pay there.

Anyhow, you have immense possibilities before you, and should be able to make something of them.

Maynard and Lucy[4] are to arrive today. Gerald is working at the right book of Adam Smith[5], after having read the wrong one on the Broads[6]. I am reading Stopford Brooke[7] on Browning. It is very elevating; such fine bracing criticism, enthusiastic appreciation of the one poet who was morally pure! Such a spirited defence of Browning's magnificent theory,

---

[1]   Goring-on-Thames, family home of Gerald Shove, where Rupert Brooke had stayed a few weeks prior to this letter. Nigel Jones, p. 264.

[2]   A reference to a line in a hymn by John Keble (1827) – "There is a book who runs may read".

[3]   Correct title *Essay on Shelley* by Robert Browning (1852).

[4]   John Maynard Keynes, Gordon Luce.

[5]   Adam Smith (1723-1790) Scottish economist.

[6]   Probably the Norfolk Broads.

[7]   Stopford Augustus Brooke (1832-1916) Irish writer. *The Poetry of Robert Browning* was published in 1902.

that God was in his heaven and all was right with the world![8]

I am amazed at the blitherings of critics. They are as bad as Browning himself, who intends to write bad poems, though they sometimes come good by chance.

And so forth.

Yours,
F. Békássy

---

[8]   Correct quotation: 'God's in His heaven/All's right with the world!' (Pippa's Song).

LETTERS TO
JAMES STRACHEY

James Strachey (1887-1967)

Strachey was the youngest son of the extensive Strachey family. He was a student at Trinity College, Cambridge, a member of the 'Apostles'. In 1909 Strachey left Cambridge to become assistant editor of the *Spectator*. At the beginning of 1914 he visited Russia, pursuing his interest in Russian theatre and ballet. Having left as a rather insignificant looking young man, while there he grew a full beard, something Békássy comments on in one of his letters to Noel. Both he and his wife Alix Sargant-Florence trained as psychoanalysts under Freud. In 1923 he became a full member of the British Psychoanalytical Society. Together with Ernest Jones and Joan Rivière, Strachey translated the complete works of Freud into English, a lifetime's work; the twenty-four volume collection remaining the standard edition of Freud's works to this day.

Brooke and Békássy did not succeeded in winning Noel Olivier's love; James Strachey (who also corresponded with her between 1911 and 1913) did, though much later: in 1932 Noel fell in love with him, beginning a long standing affair, despite the fact that they were both married.

Letter 1 to Strachey – 5 September 1912

Schluderbach
[return]address:
Kis Sennye, Rum,
Vas vm. Hungary

5 September 1912

My dear Gran'pa...[1]

I hope you thoroughly enjoyed your stay at 'The Crown Inn'.[2] I think the name of the place was [that], wasn't it? I heard you were in such excellent health, no doubt the bright sunny weather was good for you.

I have now spent nearly two weeks among these mountains, and am continually thinking how well you, who so appreciate magnificent scenery, would like it. The bold slopes, the startling light, the magnificent sunset effects suggest everything that is generously liberal; as if the very earth and sky were intent on some new, startling and noble departure - from our classical conception of nature: they strongly remind me of that magnificent Turner[3] which, if I remember, hangs above your study's mantelpiece.

But these are days of cold reason and the steady search after experience inaugurated in your time, gran'pa, and I have not merely looked at these gigantic playthings of primo(r)dial formative powers, I have ascended them. Climbed them, as you in your day have doubtless climbed many; stepping determined

'Breast and back as either should be'[4] -

---

[1]   A joke as James Strachey is merely six years older than Békássy.
[2]   The reading party at Everleigh.
[3]   Unidentified Turner painting.
[4]   Quote from *Epilogue to Asolando* (line 19) by Robert Browning.

The enthusiasm wherewith such ascents fill one is indeed comparable, is it not, to the most sublime passages in poetry; of which, (I feel sure you agree with me) this hymn of Browning is one.

Before we came away from home - I am here with my sister whom you doubtless remember, tho' she was but four years old when you last saw her - we had been living in the country, very quietly; just the humdrum family life, in which, I remember once you said, one's every virtue and vice stands out with unwonted clearness. You may well believe I enjoyed it to the full, after the wear and tear of unsettled Cambridge life. It does even a young man good sometimes to return to the family hearth, as our Lord returned to the desert, to prepare himself for the coming struggle.

But do not think that I would gladly be cut off, even for a few months, from intercourse with my English friends, therefore I have persuaded Maynard[5] to come and stay with us this September; he is not at all afraid of the dangers and the inconvenience of such a long journey and says he will certainly come. 'Honi soit qui mal y pense'[6] as French writers might say.

I must write a few words of the life I see round me, and among those of my age, - tho' they are so different from me. It is not in the nature of things that young people should possess peaceful minds; and yet so much apparently genuine, yet certainly purposeless feeling as is shown by the present generation, concerning their relations to each other, must fall[?] upon one's sense of order and decency. How very much simpler things seem to have been in gran'pa's time: now men have no great ideals to guide them, great principles are not regarded,

---

5   John Maynard Keynes.
6   'Shame on him that thinks evil of it'. French, motto of the Order of the Garter. Keynes being homosexual, Békássy must be thinking of the gossip regarding his visit to Hungary.

and there are no great men. It is as though we were waiting for the dawn; and it has not yet appeared. Darkness, however, frightens only children; it is no reason why we "young men" should despair.

I hope you will excuse me for writing so little about details, small happenings; there have been so few of them lately, and besides I felt it would be out of keeping with my surroundings, to descend to less noble topics. Are you still quite well? I hope nothing prevents you from enjoying yourself and others. I have just heard of the dreadful floods there have been;[7] but not in your parts, were they? So I have not been anxious, except of course for the nation's welfare. A hundred million tons of rain have fallen lately on the area of England: how immense are the visitations of the Divine Power!

Hoping this letter will find you in the very best of health and spirits, and in the pleasant pastime and good companie (sic) of which the poet[8] sings. I remain your most dutiful grandson

Frank

---

[7]   The 'terrible floods' in England in 1912 affected mainly Norfolk.
[8]   Referring to the poem 'Past-time with Good Company', allegedly by Henry VIII.

Letter 2 to Strachey – 20 December 1912

Petersfield, Hamps.

20 December [1912]

Dear James,

I am not going again to risk writing a letter to you which you can pretend you haven't understood! So I shall not put on any strange airs, though I might write in many different styles: as an athlete for instance; for I have been playing fives and football against my school! Or as Bedalian, since for the last few days I have been steeped in that atmosphere of petticoats and chivalry: so that I am now convinced that my body is indeed the temple of the holy spirit, and might almost put up with the ideal of Jesus the entirely human, and with broad Christianity! I have been seeing many of the people who were at school with me, and (probably because I so mismanage life) find it rather hard to talk with them, although we usually like each other. But at any rate I have seen something of the Chief[1] whom, after all, I do greatly admire. He is a thorough idealist, i.e. he can't exist for a moment without having and feeling he has an ideal (which does not prevent his being very entertaining) - and as he has made more out of his life than anyone else I know. I've never seen anyone who has been so successful.

A further complication in my state is that I am living with people whom I call Dmitri[Dimitri], or Nadejda, [Nadiezhda] Alexeievna.[2] I could give you such a nice description: 'while I am writing this, Ivan Anatolitch[3] is sitting opposite me, writing to his wife in big, bold letters.' He is a big, bold man; yet has the traditional slowness of his race... or perhaps a -

---

[1] J. H. Badley, headmaster of Bedales
[2] Nadine Jarintzoff and her son Dmitri (old Bedalian).
[3] Ivan Anatolich Jarintzoff, Dimitri's father.

psychological chapter on mother and son would be better.

It was silly of me not to have made an attempt to learn Russian, all the holidays that I spent here! I shall have to do it some time, anyhow, if only to get to know their poetry which I know is not like all this English-French-German stuff, but more like Hungarian; and my present difficulty is that as far as criticising Hungarian poetry goes I am very much at sea. It needs such different standards from the ones usually assumed in English.

I very much want to criticise, in the plodding way that I began last summer; I'm sure it's the only way to get to the real character of any poem or poet; and to do so is one of the only two things that are at all interesting. The other is of course concerned with 'aesthetic motion' - I mean some emotion one can get, by reading a poem, not towards or about it, but about life in general - or else something else in general. This emotion seems to be got by the things critics usually do talk about but I'm sure they do it in quite a mad way, and anyhow it does not seem as important as the other.

 -This, you see, is my newest small enthusiasm, but I'm afraid it isn't one at all, as I am in such a state of mind that I don't seem to care about anyone or anything. I have never been like that before, because I am not now despondent or unhappy. I do still know that everything is worth a great deal, but I don't at present think so. I suppose I am just convalescent. I am not going to recognise feeling except in its consequences. I shall never again give myself up to the wretched state I have been in for the last two years, namely of just pining away for love and not being loved. In fact:

'...I'll fling away desire, and prove
Not having known, I am not slave, to love.'[4]

---

[4]   Unknown quote, possibly his Békássy's own verse.

So to do all this, I am going to Switzerland. - I don't yet know where - I have managed to meet a Mr. Grant-Watson[5] at Montreux - all this has come quite suddenly: I am going on Saturday and knew nothing about it till a few days ago. I shall not think any more, then: I shall spend all my time skiing, and enjoying myself and Watson.

And then I shall come back, and be with my sister at the Raverats'[6] and so on; and go back to Cambridge, and work - and any little accident may put an end to all this determination of mine, and send me spinning back to where I was a week or two before the end of last term! But at any rate I shall be free while I can. I would as a matter of fact like to go further away to some - any- very warm place, if only one had the time and money. I haven't really got money enough to do this, but I can't help it, and one can always do something or other to get out of difficulties.

Isn't Ed[d]y Marsh's book[7] out yet? I ought to have got a copy long ago and it hasn't come yet. I hope it <u>will</u> come before I go!

There is a Man who lives on the top of the Hill, and his name is Edward Thomas[8] and he writes reviews and books and things. He has a Wife and two Children, and is young. I go up there some times and talk of reviews and books and things.

It was quite lucky you weren't in when I was going through London, as it was I went to Chelsea and found a lot of the sort of people who make their dresses for the Slade dance. don't know if you know them: my sister used to know them all. I was

---

[5]   Peter Grant-Watson, see Main Characters.

[6]   Probably sister Éva. For Raverats, see Main Characters.

[7]   Edward Marsh (1872-1953), Rupert Brooke's friend and literary executor, edited five volumes of *Georgian Poetry* (1912-1922). Private Secretary of Sir Winston Churchill from 1905. He was knighted for his services.

[8]   Edward Thomas, see Main Characters.

much struck by the beauty of Miss Gwendolyn Jones.[9] But I don't suppose you have ever seen her.

Write to me about you - oh, I forgot, you can't very well, as I don't yet know my address.

Yours,
Feri

[in pencil]
Of course I didn't send this off - I am now here at the Hotel Rosal, Châteaux D'Oex [sic], Switzerland till the 2ⁿᵈ [January 1913].[10] I have already managed to sprain my leg but hope it won't interfere with things. I can't write about it all now.

---

[9]   By this time Antonia, Békássy's sister had left the Slade School of Art, which she attended between 1909 and 1910. At the dance in 1912, Békássy met up with some of the friends, who were still studying there. Nothing more is known of Miss Gwendolyn Jones.

[10]   This letter written in Petersfield in England, was not posted until Békássy arrived in Switzerland.

LETTERS TO
JUSTIN BROOKE

Justin Brooke (1885-1963)

J ustin Brooke's father Arthur Brooke, (no relation to Rupert
Brooke) founded the Brooke Bond Tea Company. Justin, a
pupil at Bedales went on to Emmanuel College, Cambridge
in 1904. In 1907 he set up the Marlowe Dramatic Society
to present *Doctor Faustus*, followed by Milton's *Comus* a year
later. Together with Jacques Raverat he is thought of as one
of the leading spirits of Neo-Paganism, a movement which
also influenced the Bloomsbury Group. He was a popular
participant of Lytton Strachey's and John Maynard Keynes's
reading parties.

Békássy regarded Justin Brooke, (who visited the Békássy
family in Hungary in 1913) as one his most trusted friends.

Letter 1 – to Justin Brooke

K.C.C.

23 April 1913

Dear Justin,

I wrote to Peter[1] not long ago, so you have heard of me; but I must answer your letter. What a time you must be having and how I wish I were there too! Here? I ought to be working: but if I once work for a whole day, I am self-satisfied and do nothing for a week. The work is mostly rubbish. So of course I am not going to do well in this Tripos.[2] Next year everything I do will be interesting. The Italian renaissance for a special period!

Last hols. I plagiarised from Keats in two splendid Hungarian poems; and so I don't now think my English ones very serious.

I almost agree about the Song of Poets,[3] it might as it now stands have been written by anyone inferior: as it used to be it made false pretences, thus imposing on the credulous!

I want to do something about Adriatica; all the good parts are nothing to do with the story, which is without interest; and sodomy is absurd. There ought to be a really dramatic story to it: but what <u>can</u> happen on a sailing-yacht? I can't make them cut each other's throats! Well, if anybody wants melodrama, I have made an attempt, according to my lights. This is it:

---

[1]   Peter Grant-Watson, see Main Characters.

[2]   His second year exam.

[3]   Written by Békássy, the English version is lost. The Hungarian version 'Költők éneke' was published posthumously by his mother in 1916 and reprinted in Sennyey Weiner, pp. 142-145.

The Meditation of one sometime a lover[4]

These houses bend beneath the night
That settles on the roof
These lamps a-now bespeak delight;
But unattached, aloof

A simple stone, a grey, a cold
Oppressive tower rears
Its silence, cornered nooks enfold
The forms of many fears.

But grey they come, but they grey go,
(Pale spectres multiform)
High o'er the sky, the clouds, and slow
Pile their blockaded form

The wind his comet-course shall keep,
And bend with downward fold,
Whence warm his course arose and steep
Thither returning cold.

But faster far, but colder still
Once warm desire grows.
Pale Memory! Now neath a hill
A Husband and a Wife lies still.
Who troubles their repose?

Where is the Vale? No blessed night
Shall shroud, no fancy blind
The soul which has supplanted Sight;

---

[4]   This poem, written in iambic quatrains is a ballad in the style of the Hungarian poet János Arany (1817-1882).

Their cottage stands for ever white
Before a tortured mind.

Friend, I shall call <u>him</u> - for though frail
All feeling, Words endure.
Love, <u>her</u>: when very words shall fail,
Her image is secure.

God! There was beauty in her breath
When lips for lust grew rough;
We of sweet Living fashioned Death,
For love is not enough.

All life is harsh: a man must earn
Whatever love he can.
That share is his, nor may there yearn
For it another man.

They both, beneath the clay, to clay...
Their errant ghosts may cry;
Who killed with love their love's young day
One lives: and it is I.

Friend - for the word shall not be frail-
Come, whisper thou to me.
Come! - love and hate with life do fail:
I am no longer he.-

But grey they come, but grey they go.
Pale spectres multiform
High o'er the sky, the clouds; and slow
Pile their blockaded form.

Lately and foolishly I went to see the Jaques[es][5] without writing to them and so found Gwen but not Jaques and may have been a nuisance. It is a splendid walk though.[6] Rupert, too, I narrowly missed, but I hope I shall see him next weekend.

The chestnuts on the backs, by the way, are coming out very callously; but one can see they are only pretending not to mind!

I miss the Cornfords[7] but wish I met them in the New Forest- not near Cambridge; I wouldn't be so Cambridgeish there. But when the only way one knows people is by sitting in a room of an evening, and talking...

I wonder if you knew or know Merwyn [sic] Gotch[8] fairly well. I think he is splendid; and knows his own mind. He has tried some ten different sets in Cambridge, and not found his place among any. He has been womanising and drinking a good deal but he is almost the only Cambridge man of any interest I know who <u>lives</u> and is sane. I do admire people who always know what they want (which I do) and want what they know or can do or can get and have a place in the order of things! (which I don't).

However

yours
Feri

From your letter one thinks you are altogether well and will now remain so.[9] I do hope this is true.

---

[5] Jaques and Gwen Raverat, see Main Characters.

[6] The walk from Cambridge to Royston and the Raverats' home is described in the letter to Noel, 6 March 1913.

[7] Cornfords see Main Characters.

[8] Mervyn Gotch, ex-Bedalian, older brother of John Hugo Gotch, for latter see Main Characters.

[9] Justin Brooke suffered from nervous breakdowns, Delany, *The Neo-Pagans*, p. 223

Letter 2 to Justin Brooke – early summer 1914

King's College, Cambridge

[early summer 1914]

Dear Justin,

I write from the edge of the abyss.[10] I am going today if possible. Here are my poems - to wit, an Ode on Poetry[11] written last term, and Adriatica, begun during my May's exams last June. The Ode, of course I wrote in the wrong metre at first, and Peter[12] saw it like that, beginning

How with years has passed a silent rapture
Freer far the spirit ere it knew,
Heard entranced, attempted to recapture
All the poets sing; while fired it flew
Fast athwart the Space where Song is Motion,
Till the murmurings of many strings
Spread the ecstasy of its emotion,
Trembling with the tremor of its wings
and going on like that with great hammering.

The Adriatica - perhaps you will never speak to me again, you will think it so Cambridgey! And be annoyed at my making young men fall in love with each other? Anyhow you must put up with it. You know I sailed that way in 1907 on a yacht called the Orion, with 1/2 of my family? Which explains the descriptions. Two lines are missing somewhere because I forget the name of a bird.

Of course it is in a way rather boring, because the story has merely an equal interest all through - or almost - in spite

---

[10] Meaning leaving Cambridge for good.
[11] The poem has been lost, only the eight lines quoted in this letter survive.
[12] Peter Grant-Watson.

of Amrita.[13] I have a verdict on the poem, written after I had
abandoned the attempt in June. It is in deliberate imitation of
Browning. And runs:-

Ah well! Bury you, throw you over?
Jilt you, my love, your only lover?
-Knowing you thorough, [sic] cover to cover…
Rot and crumble! Too passionate rover
I, to follow such trashy fancy,
Overmuch steeped in necromancy!

Ah well! - Cry off another attempt!
Little is lost, as little meant;
Pity though: surely that was my bent!
-High ambition is impotent:
Adjectives, speeches, paper and ink-
Men too? —You can't have everything!

Excuse my not writing more and don't lose my precious
TREASURE. My BOOK of POETRY![14] Though I'm in no
hurry for it.

Yours
Feri.

I wish (almost) that I wasn't going home: I might stay with
you and with the Jaques' —but then, to be away from England!

---

13 Amrita, Sanskrit word meaning 'nectar', name of one of the characters in the
    poem 'Adriatica', also the title of a separate poem in Hungarian, a fictionalised
    version of Noel Olivier. The poem translated into English is included in this
    volume (Amrita says, p. 55).
14 Probably a notebook of his own handwritten poems in English, as one exists in
    Hungarian.

LETTERS TO
CONSTANCE GARNETT

Constance Garnett (1861-1946)

B orn and educated in Brighton, in 1879 when it was still unusual for women to go into higher education, Constance Garnett won a scholarship to Newnham College, Cambridge. She married the critic Edward Garnett and after becoming friends in London with Russian exiles she began to translate from the Russian. She travelled to Russia several times and visited Leo Tolstoy. Altogether she translated over 70 books including works by Chekhov, Dostoevsky, Turgenev and Tolstoy.

She lived near Limpsfield where the Olivier family resided and Békássy became acquainted with her through her son David (Bunny) Garnett, a childhood friend of Noel Olivier.

Letter 1 to Constance Garnett – 7 July 1914

38 Brunswick Square
Tel: 7267 City WC

7 July 1914

Dear Mrs. Garnett,[1]

I hope you will not mind my writing to you, and will not think it presumptuous of me to say how much I wish that you could translate a book I have come across lately. The book is Ключи Счастья,[2] А. Вербицкой,[3] and although I cannot read Russian properly, a lady[4] with whom I was staying translated many scenes to me out of it, and told me the story of the plot. (It is a novel of great length and crowded with all kind of riches.) The book has been coming out for the last three years and its publication is now completed. I feel very enthusiastic about it, and am almost sure that it must be a very good book. It is written in a very unusual style: scenes dramatic and vivid from half a page to four or five pages in length; and, it seems to me written with great wit and wisdom and feeling. They say that the book reflects all that is best in the last ten years of Russian activity. At any rate it contains an enormous mass and variety of scenes and characters. *The Keys of Happiness* are concerned with love and freedom, all from the woman's point of view; one girl, though she holds them in her hands, cannot keep them, and the book ends in tragedy. For some time I thought it might be both melodramatic and *Tendenz*[5] literature, but I think it is neither. The writer's knowledge

---

[1] This letter was sent to the wrong address and forwarded to the Garnetts' home in Edenbridge.
[2] *Keys to Happiness.*
[3] Anastasia Verbitzkaya.
[4] Nadine Jarintzoff.
[5] Partisan or biased angle in a literary work.

of human feelings has helped her out of this, and her feeling that after all, nothing as important as human relationships (individual relations) has transformed her leaning towards the other. The characters and the great scenes are such as one does not find outside Dostoevsky, though of course the style is not so simple nor so incisive and is sometimes on the verge of being florid. The method of building up a novel out of detached consecutive scenes first interested me - it is rather like some of Rainer Maria Rilke's[6] books, (though on a different scale.) Do you think you could read it? It would at any rate not be a waste of time; and perhaps you would then translate it. No doubt a horrible German translation will be made soon, but in English it might be a translation with real literary merit, at any rate if you translate it. It is a book that must have great influence on people.

Please excuse this intrusion - I cannot master my enthusiasm and my hopes-

Yours very sincerely.
F. Békássy

---

[6]   Rainer Maria Rilke (1875-1926) Austrian poet and prose-writer.

Letter 2 to Constance Garnett – 29 July 1914

Kis-Sennye

Wednesday 29 July 1914

Dear Mrs. Garnett,

Many thanks for your kind letter… Of course Dostoevsky and Chehov [sic] have prior claims: but I still have some hope; four years is not so long, after all!

I'm afraid I can't get hold of the book very easily (at present I hope you will get even this letter safely!) but I hope you will read the rest of it.

I'm afraid too, that I have left England, and I don't know <u>when</u> I shall be back there[1]. It may be quite soon, in two years or three. But of course you have read about the war; so one isn't very confident in making forecasts. At present, I am not going but <u>if</u> all our troops are mobilised probably I too will have to go, first to learn for some four weeks and then (if it lasts) to the war. I won't myself mind going: but it's worse for some of the people who stay at home. Of course half our relations are soldiers and have gone, or may go - you can imagine the state we are all in, anxiety, turmoil; and enthusiasm (where many people are together.) it is a bad business, but there is something to be gained from it, even for the country - not only for individuals.

Yours sincerely

F. Békássy

I am sorry I could not see David[2] at all this summer; please give him my love and best wishes.- Even apart from the war, I don't know how I would return; I see I am getting stuck in the soil already. It's a deadly place, Hungary, - when one likes it so.

---

[1] In fact, we know that in the beginning of August Békássy returned to England to fetch his sisters. See Introduction.

[2] Constance Garnett's son David.

IN MEMORIAM

Féri Bekassy [1] *by Frances Cornford*

We, who must grow old and staid,
Full of wisdom, much afraid,
In our hearts like flowers keep
Love for you until you sleep.

You the brave, and you the young
You of thousand songs unsung,
Burning brain, and ardent word,
You the lovely and absurd.

Say, on that Galician plain
Are you arguing again?
Does a trench or ruined tree
Hear your - 'O, I don't agree!'

We, who must grow staid and old,
Full of caution, worn and cold,
In our hearts, like flowers keep,
Your image, till we also sleep.

1915

---

[1] correct spelling 'Feri Békássy'

A letter from Gordon Luce to
John Maynard Keynes (excerpt)

15 March 1916

-Tell me all you can about Feri's death. Our intimacy had richly developed since I came to Burma, and I am left with a pile of glorious letters, MS-poems, and what not. I mention this in case Adriatica is published. (I have variations on its finale etc.). I admire the poetry of none of us like his, 'proud with the proud reality of thought.' Was he patriotic at all, and if so, a Magyar of the Kossuth[1] type, perhaps? Or, as I suspect, utterly at a loss and shuddering? For conviction and happiness came to him only after long hours of thought. I have written many poems of vulgar rage over his death, but destroyed them all wisely. Now I am engaged on an elaboration of some lines I once sent you, beginning 'Would I could parley with a temperate man,'[2] which, in the first instance I wrote in reach at a man combining your qualities and his. His spell I remember more potent than anyone's on Sat. nights, his words fluent and rich, yet troubled, like the pool of Bethesda.[3]

---

[1] Lajos Kossuth (1802-1894) Hungarian political reformer who led the Hungarian struggle for Independence from Austria in 1848-1849. After its failure, he fled to Turkey, then lived in emigration in England and later in Italy where he died.

[2] The poem from which he quotes is now lost.

[3] Biblical pool near Jerusalem. The Angel of the Lord would occasionally descend and stir the water. The first ill person to jump in would be healed, John 5:2.

The memorial in King's College Chapel to Kingsmen who were killed in the First World War contains the name of Rupert Brooke but not of Ferenc Békássy. Later, a plaque commemorating Békássy's death was placed next to the main memorial. (The word 'Pensioner' refers to the fact that Békássy was a fee-paying student rather than a scholar.) This photo was taken in June 2015, the hundredth anniversary of Békássy's death, when a wreath was placed there by visitors from Békássy's village.

EPILOGUE –
THE ALIEN IN THE CHAPEL

Peter Jones, Fellow Librarian,
King's College, Cambridge

The commemoration of Ferenc Békássy's death in action was never going to be straightforward for King's College. His attachment to the place and his many friends there pulled in one direction; the grief for other young men killed while serving on the opposing side pulled in another.

In the course of the First World War King's College lost nearly 23% of its members serving in the armed forces (774 in total).[1] The College had emptied rapidly by 1915 as so many had volunteered to fight. Those that remained could not but be reminded of their losses as they began rapidly to mount. The empty rooms left in the College were filled with nurses working in the First Eastern General Hospital which had opened in 1914 on the former College sports fields. Ferenc Békássy 's death was noticed in the College's Annual Report

---

[1] Tomás Irish, "Fractured Families: Educated Elites in Britain and France and the Challenge of the Great War", *Historical Journal* 57 (2014), 509-30 (525).

for 1915, published in November that year:

> Ferinc (sic) Békássy, son of Stephen Békássy of
> Kis Sennye, Szombathely, Hungary, graduated in
> History in 1914. He was called up for training
> in the Hungarian army and eventually sent to the
> front in the Bukowina, where he fell in June 1915.
> The College loses in him a man of great goodness
> of character and intellectual promise. He is deeply
> regretted by his many English friends.[2]

In the same issue appeared a more extravagant tribute to Rupert Brooke, his fellow poet, also killed in action, but already granted the status of a national hero following tributes paid in the newspapers by the Dean of St Paul's (a Kingsman) and Winston Churchill. More recently, on 13 October 1915, a third young poet, Charles Hamilton Sorley, had been killed by a sniper during the battle of Loos.[3] He had not been a King's undergraduate, but had been a pupil at the King's Choir School. His father was William Ritchie Sorley, Knightbridge Professor of Moral Philosophy at the University of Cambridge, and a Fellow of King's since 1901. This last poet's death in 1915 was to have a big impact on the commemoration of Békássy in King's College.

John Maynard Keynes, who had become Second Bursar at King's in 1919, was appointed to the Committee set up by the College to devise an appropriate memorial for the College's war dead. The Committee was chaired by the Provost, Walter Durnford, and the other influential member was the Dean of Chapel, Eric Milner-White.[4] Milner-White had returned to

---

[2] King's College Annual Report (1915), p. 8.
[3] Michael De-la-Noy, 'Sorley, Charles Hamilton (1895–1915)', rev. *Oxford Dictionary of National Biography*, Oxford University Press, 2004; online edn, Jan 2012 [http://www.oxforddnb.com/view/article/37996, accessed 16 Feb 2016].
[4] King's College Archive Centre, Cambridge, Governing records, KCGB/4/1/1/12, 25 October 1919.

England after serving as a chaplain to the forces at the western front and in Italy; he had been awarded the DSO for his service as senior chaplain and combatant officer in the 7th division in 1917. He had lost his dearest friend at the front. Appointed a Fellow and Dean of Chapel at King's in 1918 (he had been chaplain at King's before the war), Milner-White instituted the famous service of Nine Lessons and Carols at King's the same year.[5] Milner-White was passionately committed to renewing the liturgy in the Chapel and to the continuing adornment of a unique building. The Committee for the war memorial to which Keynes and Milner-White were appointed reported back in February 1920 and suggested the use of the south-eastern side chapel of King's College Chapel as a dedicated memorial chapel. Keynes had argued that there should be a monument recording the names of the dead in the main Chapel but he was outvoted.[6]

The design of the memorial chapel was entrusted to the Cambridge architect T.H. Lyon, who was to be responsible also for war memorials in Pembroke and Sidney Sussex Colleges. The plan was to inscribe the names of the fallen on the inner wall of the side chapel, while Lyon designed an altarpiece in stone at the eastern end, and Milner-White filled the exterior wall glass with the Holy Hunt, a beautiful German composition of the early sixteenth century, given by Mrs Laurence Humphry in memory of her husband, and with his own donation of some nearly contemporary glass portraying Old Testament Kings.[7] He recorded his war service as a chaplain with an inscription and badges in small modern quarries of glass at the bottom of

---

[5] Natalie K. Watson, 'White, Eric Milner- (1884–1963)', *Oxford Dictionary of National Biography*, Oxford University Press, 2004; online edn, May 2008 [http://www.oxforddnb.com/view/article/47849, accessed 16 Feb 2016].

[6] King's College Archive Centre, Congregation Book, KCGB/4/1/1/12, 14 February 1920.

[7] King's College Annual Report (1920), p. 11.

the Old Testament Kings window.[8]

Keynes wanted a simple design for the memorial inscription on the wall, listing the fallen in their order of precedence in the College, from Fellows through Scholars and Pensioners and ultimately to members of the Choir School and College servants.[9] He suggested it should have an English superscription, but the Provost argued that such a thing in an ecclesiastical building must be in Latin, and so it reads today '1914 Quasi Morientes Et Ecce Vivimus 1919' ('As dying and behold we live').[10] The Lyon designs for the Memorial Chapel were approved by the College in October 1920.[11] The cost was to be met by an appeal to members of the College and the relatives of those who had died. Keynes subscribed £100 to the War Memorial Fund himself, one of the largest single donations.[12]

One feature of the design caused controversy within the College. The original design for the wall inscription had made room at the bottom right for a special ruled compartment below the list of College Servants, within which was to appear the name of Ferenc Békássy, Pensioner.[13] It seems that opposition to the inclusion of Békássy's name on the wall was led by W.R. Sorley, father of the poet C.H. Sorley, whose name was originally to appear in the same column of the memorial as that of Békássy. Evidently Sorley senior was affronted that the name of one of those who had fought as an enemy to his son

---

[8]   Hilary Wayment, *King's College Chapel Cambridge: The Side-Chapel Glass* (Cambridge: Cambridge Antiquarian Society and the Provost and Scholars of King's College, Cambridge, 1988), pp. 143-52.

[9]   Ross Harrison, *Our College Story: A short history of the King's College of St Nicholas and Our Lady in Cambridge* (Cambridge: King's College, Cambridge, 2015), p. 101.

[10] King's College Archive Centre, Cambridge: Papers of John Maynard Keynes, JMK/KC/5/1/33, W. Durnford to Keynes 28 February 1921.

[11] King's College Archive Centre, Congregation Book, KCGB/4/1/1/12, 30 October 1920.

[12] War Memorial Subscription List, November 1922: King's College Archive Centre, KCAR/3/1/2/4/8, p. 144.

[13] King's College Archive Centre, Cambridge, KCC/626.

should appear at all on this memorial to the dead of King's. Sorley's role in this affair was later remarked on by Ludwig Wittgenstein, who told a Dutch friend O. K. Bouwsma about it. Wittgenstein reported that a 'professor of ethics', no less, had objected to commemorating a Hungarian student amongst the dead of his own College (wrongly identified as Christ's).[14] The College's own records are silent on the subject of the dispute in the Fellowship. Keynes suggested the eventual compromise solution, inscribing Békássy's name not on the inner wall but on the section of wall by the door to the Chapel, at right angles to the inner wall. This is where Békássy's memorial at King's is still to be seen.

The War Memorial Chapel was dedicated on 2 November 1921 by the Bishop of Lincoln, the College's Visitor. The order of service was arranged by Milner-White; three poems of Rupert Brooke were read, and one by C. H. Sorley. Unsurprisingly, perhaps, given the controversy, no poem of Békássy was read.[15] The War Memorial Fund was very much oversubscribed after the bills for the Memorial Chapel had been paid, and in June 1922 the unexpended funds were transferred to a War Memorial Educational Fund, giving grants to sons and relatives of King's men who had fallen in the war, and to sons and others not able to afford university education as a result of the war.[16]

In 1925 Keynes helped fund another published memorial to Ferenc Békássy. A selection of his poems in English, introduced by his fellow Apostle and King's Fellow, F.L (Peter) Lucas, was published at the Hogarth Press as *Adriatica*. The Hogarth

---

[14] Michael Nedo and Michele Ranchetti (ed.), *Ludwig Wittgenstein: sein Leben in Bildern und Texten* (Frankfurt am Main: Suhrkamp, 1983), pp. 144-5, p. 371; L.P. Wilkinson, *Kingsmen of a Century 1873-1972* (Cambridge: King's College, Cambridge, 1981), 279.

[15] King's College Archive Centre, CSV/50.

[16] King's College Annual Report (1922), p. 10.

Press was run by Leonard and Virginia Woolf, close friends of Keynes, who had in fact brought Békássy to stay at their house at Asheham in Sussex before the war.

After W. R. Sorley died in 1935 his widow gave a cubical sundial to King's College to commemorate him. It had stood originally at the Church of St Anne on the Sands, Dunbar, and one part of it dates from 1649. The sundial was placed in 1938 close to the south-east corner of the Chapel, standing on grass inside the Wilkins Screen. Sorley's memorial is thus no more than a few feet from the inscription in the War Memorial Chapel recording his son's death in 1915.[17]

On 1 June 2015 a wreath in Hungarian national colours was placed by the citizens of Szombathely, Hungary, on the Békássy memorial to mark the centenary of his death.[18]

---

[17] *An Inventory of the Historical Monuments in the City of Cambridge, Part I* (London: Royal Commission on Historical Monuments England, 1959), p. 131.

[18] I should like to thank Dr Patricia McGuire, Archivist of King's College, Cambridge, for her invaluable help with College records in preparing this Epilogue.

BIBLIOGRAPHY

Ferenc Békássy in English

Basileon 'Sonnet' and 'Adventurer', June 1913, 'Hoc erat in votis' June 1914

Békássy, Ferenc, *Adriatica and other poems*, Hogarth Press, London, 1925. The two excerpts in this volume are from Adriatica, Chapter II (Off Incoronata)

Copp, Michael, ed., the poem '1914' in *Cambridge Poets of the Great War*, Madison-Teaneck, Farleigh Dickinson University, 2001, pp. 127-128

Gál, István, 'A Hungarian at King's', *The New Hungarian Quarterly*, No.41, Spring 1971, pp.188-191

Gömöri, George, 'Ferenc Békássy's letters to John Maynard Keynes', *The New Hungarian Quarterly*, No.79, Autumn 1980, pp. 159-170

Gömöri, George, 'Ferenc Békássy, Rupert Brooke and Noel Olivier' *Hungarian Quarterly*, No.199, Vol.51, Autumn 2010. Two of Ferenc Békássy's letters to Noel Olivier are printed in the Appendix to the article. pp.105-113

Gömöri, George, 'Ferenc Békássy, Rupert Brooke and Noel Olivier', *The Rupert Brooke Society Journal*, Winter 2011-2012, pp. 20-33

Gömöri, George, 'Ferenc Békássy's Correspondence with James Strachey', *Hungarian review*, Vol.IV. No.3, May 2013, pp.76-80

Gömöri, George, 'Letters of John Maynard Keynes from Hungary and Vienna', *Hungarian review*, Vol.VI. No. 6, December 2015, pp.20-24

Potter, Caroline, Dr. 'The King's Hussar: Ferenc Békássy and the Great War', www.asketchofthepast.com 15 March 2015

Sherwood, Peter, An Introduction to the poem '1914' ed., Tim Cross *The Lost Voices of World War I*, Bloomsbury, London, 1988, pp. 346-347.

Szirtes, George, georgeszirtes.blogspot.com, 'A Note on Ferenc Békássy', 4 January 2014

Tillyard, Aelfrida ed., *Cambridge Poets 1900-1913*, Heffers and Sons, Cambridge, 1913, pp. 17-19

Weiner Sennyey, Tibor ed., *Békássy Ferenc egybegyűjtött írásai*, (The collected writings of Ferenc Békássy) Aranymadár, Budapest-Zsennye, 2010

SOURCES

Primary sources

Ferenc Békássy to Noel Olivier, Tamsin Majerus, Nottingham

Ferenc Békássy to John Maynard Keynes, Archives Centre, King's College, Cambridge, PP/JMK/PP/45/1-31

Ferenc Békássy to John T. Sheppard, Archives Centre, King's College, Cambridge, JTS//PP/2/13

Ferenc Békássy to James Strachey, British Library, MS Additional 60568

Ferenc Békássy to Justin Brooke, Elizabeth Hollingsworth, Bury St Edmunds

Ferenc Békássy to Constance Garnett, Special Collection, Charles Deering and McCormick Library, Northwestern University, Evanston, Illinois, MS 164

Gordon Luce to John Maynard Keynes, Archives Centre, King's College, Cambridge, JMK/PP/45/193/151

John Maynard Keynes to Duncan Grant, British Library, MS Additional 57931

Secondary sources

Fodor, Tünde/ Topolay, Ágnes, eds. , *Babits Mihály levelezése,1914-1916*, Argumentum, Budapest, 2008

Bedales Chronicle, 1910-1914

Bedales Records, 1914-1915

Brabant, Eva, Falzeder, Ernst, and Giamperi-Deutsch, Patrizia, eds, *The Correspondence of Sigmund Freud, Szándor Ferenczi, Vol. 2: 1914-1919*, Harvard University Press, 1993

Cornford, Frances, *Collected Poems*, Cresset Press, London, 1954

Cross, Tim ed., *The Lost Voices of World War I.* Bloomsbury, London, 1988

Davenport-Hines, Richard, *Universal Man. The Seven Lives of John Maynard Keynes*, William Collins, London, 2015

Delany, Paul, *The Neo-Pagans, Friendship and Love in the Rupert Brooke Circle*, A Hamish Hamilton Paperback, London, 1987

Delany, Paul, *Fatal Glamour. The Life of Rupert Brooke*, McGill-Queens University Press, Montreal and Kingston, Ithaca, 2015

Falkiner, Suzanne, *The Imago, E.L. Grant-Watson and Australia*, UWA Publishing, Western Australia, Crawley, 2011

Fermor, Patrick Leigh, *Between the Water and the Woods*, John Murray, London, 1986

Gál, István, *Babits Mihály*, Argumentum, Budapest, 2008

Garnett, David, *The Golden Echo*, Chatto & Windus, London, 1953

Garnett, Richard, *Constance Garnett. A Heroic Life*, Sinclair-Stevenson, London, 1991

Gömöri, György, Weiner Sennyey, Tibor, eds., *Békássy Ferenc szerelmes levelei*, Aranymadár alapítvány, Budapest - Zsennye, 2013

Grant Watson, E.L. *But to What Purpose, The Autobiography of a Contemporary*, The Cresset Press, London, 1946

Hale, Keith, ed., *Friends and Apostles, The Correspondence of Rupert Brooke and James Strachey, (1905-1914)*, Yale University Press, New York and London, 1998

Harris, Pippa ed., *Song of Love, The Letters of Rupert Brooke and Noel Olivier 1909-1915*, Bloomsbury, London, 1999

Harrod, R.F., *The Life of John Maynard Keynes*, Penguin, Harmondsworth, 1951

Hassall, Christopher, *Rupert Brooke: A Biography*,2nd ed. Faber and Faber, London, 1972

Hollis, Matthew, ed.,*Thomas, Edward, Selected Poems*, Faber and Faber, London, 2014

Holroyd, Michael, *Lytton Strachey: A Biography*. Penguin, Harmondsworth, 1971

Jones, Ernest, *Sigmund Freud, Life and Work, Years of Maturity 1901-1919*, Hogarth Press, London, 1958.

Jones, Nigel, *Rupert Brooke, Life, Death and Myth*, Richard Cohen Books, London, 1999.

Keynes, Geoffrey, ed. *The Letters of Rupert Brooke* Faber & Faber, London, 1968.

Knight, Sarah, *Bloomsbury Outsider, A Life of David Garnett*, Bloomsbury Reader, London, 2015.

Levy, Paul, *Moore: G.E. Moore and the Cambridge Apostles*, Weidenfeld and Nicholson, London,1979

Lubenow, W.C., *The Cambridge Apostles, 1820-1914*, Cambridge University Press, Cambridge, 1998

Mann, Sheila, *Aelfrida Tillyard, Hints of a Perfect Splendour, A Novel Biography*, [Cambridge], 2013

Marsh, Edward ed., *The Collected Poems of Rupert Brooke: With a Memoir*, Sidgwick and Jackson Ltd., London, 1929

Proctor, D. ed., *The Autobiography of Goldsworthy Lowes Dickinson*, Duckworth, London, 1975

Read, Mike, *Forever England. The Life of Rupert Brooke*, Mainstream Publishing, Edinburgh, 1997

Shils, Edward/Blacker, Carmen eds., *Cambridge Women*, Cambridge University Press, Cambridge, 1996

Spalding, Frances, *Duncan Grant*, Chatto & Windus, London, 1997

Spalding, Frances, *Gwen Raverat, Friends, Family and Affections*, The Harvill Press, London, 2001

Spalding, Frances, *The Bloomsbury Group*, National Portrait Gallery, London, 2005

Strachan, Hew, *The First World War*, Simon & Schuster, London, 2014

Turnbaugh, Douglas Blair, *Duncan Grant and the Bloomsbury Group*, Bloomsbury, London, 1987

Wake, Roy and Denton, Pennie, *Bedales School. The First Hundred Years,1893-1993*, Haggerston Press, London, 1993

Weiner Sennyey, Tibor, ed., *Békássy Ferenc egybegyűjtött írásai*, Aranymadár alapítvány-Irodalmi jelen, Budapest-Zsennye, 2010

EDITORS' BIOGRAPHIES

George Gömöri

George Gömöri is a Hungarian poet and translator living in London. In 1956 as a fourth year student of Polish at the University of Budapest, and already a published poet, he was one of the students who organised the student march (in support of the Polish demands for reform), which escalated into the Hungarian Revolution. He had to leave Hungary and finished his studies at St. Antony's College, Oxford. He was lecturer in Polish and Hungarian Literature at Cambridge University for 32 years and is now Emeritus Fellow of Darwin College. He has published over fifty books, a dozen books of poetry in Hungarian, four in English and one in Polish, as well as several collections of essays on modern Polish and Hungarian literature as well as on Anglo-Hungarian relations.

He is a member of the Polish Academy of Arts and Sciences (Cracow) and an External Member of the Hungarian Academy of Science. His last two books in English, published in 2013, were a collection of essays, *The Polish Swan Triumphant*, and a book of poems, *Polishing October*. He was made Commander of the Order of Merit of the Hungarian Republic in 2007. His literary prizes include the Salvatore Quasimodo Prize, 1993, the Ada Negri Prize, 1995, the Pro Cultura Hungarica ,1999 and in 2014, the Janus Pannonius Translation Prize. In 2006, for his wife Mari's 60th birthday he published *Poems for Mari*, a collection of the poems he had written to her over the years.

Mari Markus Gömöri

Mari Gömöri, née Markus, came to England with her family after the 1956 Hungarian Revolution when she was ten years old. She trained at the Royal Academy of Dramatic Art and worked for ATV television. She became Director of her family business, Markus Coffee Company, when her father died. After marrying George in 1981 she moved to Cambridge and started the Mari Markus Gomori Concerts for Children, a series which ran for twenty years. *The Alien in the Chapel* is the second book George and Mari have edited together, the first one being *I Lived on this Earth...* an anthology of Hungarian poets on the Holocaust, 2012. George and Mari now live in London and have five children and five grandchildren.

INDEX

Ferenc Békássy and Noel Olivier are referred to as "FB" and "NO" in index entries

C